URBAN TRAVEL GUIDE
NEW YORK

urban travel guide - new york, isbn 90 5767 138 7
© mo' media, breda, the netherlands, 2004

All rights reserved. No part of this guide may be reproduced, stored in a retrieval system or made public in any form or by any means, electronic, mechanical or otherwise, without the prior written permission of the publisher.

COLOPHON

AUTHOR zahra sethna **FINAL EDITING** alex tobin **PHOTOGRAPHY** rené clement **GRAPHIC DESIGN** mattmo concept | design, amsterdam **CARTOGRAPHY** eurocartografie, hendrik-ido-ambacht **PROJECT GUIDANCE** joyce enthoven, renée ter berg & marty van rijen, mo' media

This guide has been compiled with the utmost care. Mo' Media BV cannot be held liable in the case of any inaccuracies within the text. Any remarks or comments should be directed to the following address.

mo' media, p.o. box 7028, 4800 ga, breda, the netherlands, e-mail info@momedia.nl

PREFACE

They say you either love New York or hate it. For me it's a bit of both. New Yorkers can be abrasive, aggressive and downright rude. But they can also be charming, impulsive and very funny. New York just wouldn't be the same place without these characters and I certainly wouldn't like it as much.

Try to see as much of New York as you can on your visit – from the outside and the inside. Get off the main avenues and away from the tourist throngs for a sense of how people really live. You'll find most New Yorkers to be very approachable, so don't be shy about asking for directions or advice.

Physically, the city is striking. In **Points of View** you'll find suggestions for getting your fill of its iconic landmarks. **NYC 24/7** outlines a unique New York phenomenon – the acronym – while taking you to some of the city's hippest hangouts.

Check out **Star Gazing** for pointers on some of the places celebrities like best or **Ethni-city** for a tour of the multicultural sights, sounds and tastes of the city. Experience what it's like to be **Single in the City**, take a musical journey through **Groovin' Gotham**, and tend to your **Body and Soul** in true Manhattan style. If you're in a hurry, we'll show you how to see **NYC in 20 stops**.

It would take several lifetimes to experience all of New York. But with this guide you can see enough to understand why New Yorkers call their city the Capital of the World.

Zahra Sethna

Zahra Sethna hunted the streets of the city in search of the best adresses.

René Clement, photograher, gives you a sneak preview of New York.

CONTENTS

3	**PREFACE**
5	**HOW TO USE THIS GUIDE**
6	**PRACTICAL INFORMATION**
8	**POINTS OF VIEW** Best ways to see the city
30	**NYC 24/7** From SoHa to BoCoCa
50	**STAR GAZING** A fixation for fame and fortune
78	**ETHNI-CITY** The Great Melting Pot
104	**SINGLE IN THE CITY** Meet your Match
130	**GROOVIN' GOTHAM** Where musical history is made
156	**BODY & SOUL** Pamper yourself
180	**NYC IN 20 STOPS** Take a bite out of the Big Apple
206	**MAPS**
214	**CATEGORY INDEX**
216	**ALPHABETICAL INDEX**
222	**SUBWAY**

HOW TO USE THIS GUIDE

In this guide we list the best addresses in New York for shopping, dining and drinking, as well as nightlife, lodging, culture and other sights of interest. Each address has a number; you'll find these numbers both on the map at the beginning of each chapter and on the detailed maps at the end of the guide. For each address, a letter indicates on which detailed map you can find it. The number on the map corresponds to the page number of the address (in the example below, South Street Seaport would be on page 14). We've also used colors to indicate the different categories:

- 🟢 shopping
- 🟠 food & drink
- 🟠 nightlife
- 🟡 lodging
- 🟣 culture
- 🔵 various

Example: number 14, map F, **SOUTH STREET SEAPORT**
You can find the address of South Street Seaport on the map at the beginning of 'Points of view' and on the more detailed map B at the end of the guide. Number 14 is green, which means this is a shop.

PRICE INDICATION FOR HOTELS AND RESTAURANTS
The prices listed are average prices for entrées (main course) in restaurants, cocktails in bars, etc. For hotels, the price listed is the starting rate for a double room per night, but keep in mind that this is the published rate – with a few mouse clicks or phone calls, you should be able to get a better rate.

DO YOU HAVE ANY SUGGESTIONS FOR US?
We've tried to compile this guide with the utmost care. However, addresses change, prices go up and phone numbers get disconnected. Should you no longer be able to find a certain address or have other comments or suggestions for us concerning this guide, please let us know. You'll find our address on page 2.

PRACTICAL INFORMATION

Transportation
The fastest way to get around the city is by subway. The bus system is also good, though due to traffic it can be slower. Although trains and buses run all night, it's a good idea to take a taxi after 11pm.

Buses and subways charge $2 per ride, payable with pay-per-use or unlimited-ride MetroCard cards. A $15 pay-per-use card offers 11 trips for the price of 10, while unlimited-ride cards come in three amounts: a 1-day Fun Pass ($7), a 7-day pass ($21) and a 30-day pass ($70). These are good for unlimited rides during that time period, but can only be used once every 18 minutes and only by one person at a time.

Taxis are available when the center light on top of the car is lit. The average fare for a three-mile (4,5 km) trip is between $5 and $7, depending on traffic and time of day. It's customary to tip the driver about a dollar or, if the fare is high, about 15%.

A cab is the most direct way to travel to and from the airports, but it will cost you about $20 or $50, depending on the airport you need to get to. A more affordable option is to make use of a direct coach service such as the New York Airport Service Express or the Newark Airport Express. This will cost you around $10 to $12 per person. The buses depart regularly, from early in the morning until about 11pm.

Useful addresses
OFFICIAL VISITOR INFORMATION CENTER ADDRESS 810 seventh avenue
TELEPHONE 212 484 1222

Useful websites
TOURIST INFO www.nycvisit.com
PUBLIC TRANSPORTATION www.mta.nyc.ny.us
TRANSPORTATION TO AND FROM AIRPORT www.nyairportservice.com, www.olympiabus.com
HOTELS www.hotels-in-new-york-online.com
NIGHTLIFE www.nyclubs.com

Public holidays
New Year's Day — 1 January
Martin Luther King Jr. Day — third Monday in January
President's Day — third Monday in February
Memorial Day — last Monday in May
Independence Day — 4 July
Labor Day — first Monday in September
Columbus Day — second Monday in October
Veteran's Day — 11 November
Thanksgiving — fourth Thursday in November
Christmas — 25 December

shopping　　food & drink　　nightlife　　lodging　　culture　　various

POINTS OF VIEW

BEST WAYS TO SEE THE CITY

"Manhattan has been compelled to **expand skyward** because of the absence of any other direction in which to grow. This, more than any other thing, is responsible for its **physical majesty**," wrote author E.B. White. "It is to the nation what the white church spire is to the village – the visible symbol of **aspiration and faith**, the white plume saying that the way is up."

White's words are as true now as they were when he wrote them in 1948. The sight of Manhattan's soaring skyscrapers and bustling, busy streets is synonymous the world over with power, **success** and **wealth**.

If asked, most people can call to mind an **image of Manhattan** without trouble, regardless of whether or not they've ever visited the city. They have seen it hundreds, perhaps thousands of times in their lives – in commercials, on television, in movies, in photos. They've heard it described in song, fiction and verse, heard other people speak of it, seen postcards, paintings and posters of it. Only a handful of other cities are so iconic, so **instantly recognizable**.

When you get to New York, whether it's your first trip or your 50th, you can't help being **energized** by the **skyline**. That panoramic view of twinkling lights, soaring buildings and elegant bridges is the **essence** of being in

shopping   food & drink   nightlife   lodging   culture   various

New York. For many, that sight simply means being home; for others it elicits excitement, opportunity, romance and adventure.

In the 1800s, **church steeples and ships' masts** were the major vertical punctuations on the skyline of the city. Homes were mostly made of wood and brick and were rarely more than two or three levels. When City Hall was built in the 1820s, it dominated the landscape.

By the 1850s, the city's population had surpassed the **half-million** mark. To keep pace with this population growth, construction stretched north of 14th Street. The intersection of 5th Avenue and 42nd Street was, at that time, considered the northern edge of the city. New Yorkers used to travel there to take **Sunday strolls** along the walls of the massive distributing tank that housed the city's reservoir of water and enjoy views of the **city** below.

It was only a matter of years before growth along 5th Avenue continued past 42nd Street. **Elegant homes** and rows of houses replaced the shantytowns, livestock pens, slaughterhouses and garbage dumps that had once littered the area. In the late 1850s, the city's *Evening Standard* newspaper reported that, "The rapid growth of New York has ceased to be a matter of astonishment." By 1864, half the city's population lived **north of 14th Street** and by 1867 the northern boundary of the city had reached 59th Street.

The modern skyline is **still in flux** just as it was when the city was first founded. Most recently Manhattan's skyline dramatically changed after September 11, 2001, when it lost two of its tallest skyscrapers. But in typically resilient style the **city has bounced back** and is rebuilding and adding new additions to the landscape.

Some of the **best vantage points** from which to see the city are from the top of the Empire State Building, from a Circle Line tour of the island, from the Staten Island Ferry or from the Brooklyn Heights Promenade. The best views, of course, are on **sunny days**, especially in the early morning or late afternoon. Nighttime views are most stunning during the week, when night crews keep the **lights** on in **office buildings** as they are cleaning.

It has been said that you can tell **Manhattan tourists** from a mile away because they're the ones always **looking up**. Don't let this deter you. As a visitor you are allowed, perhaps even compelled, to spend some time standing on the sidewalk **staring up**. It's really quite a sight, so take it all in.

POINTS OF VIEW

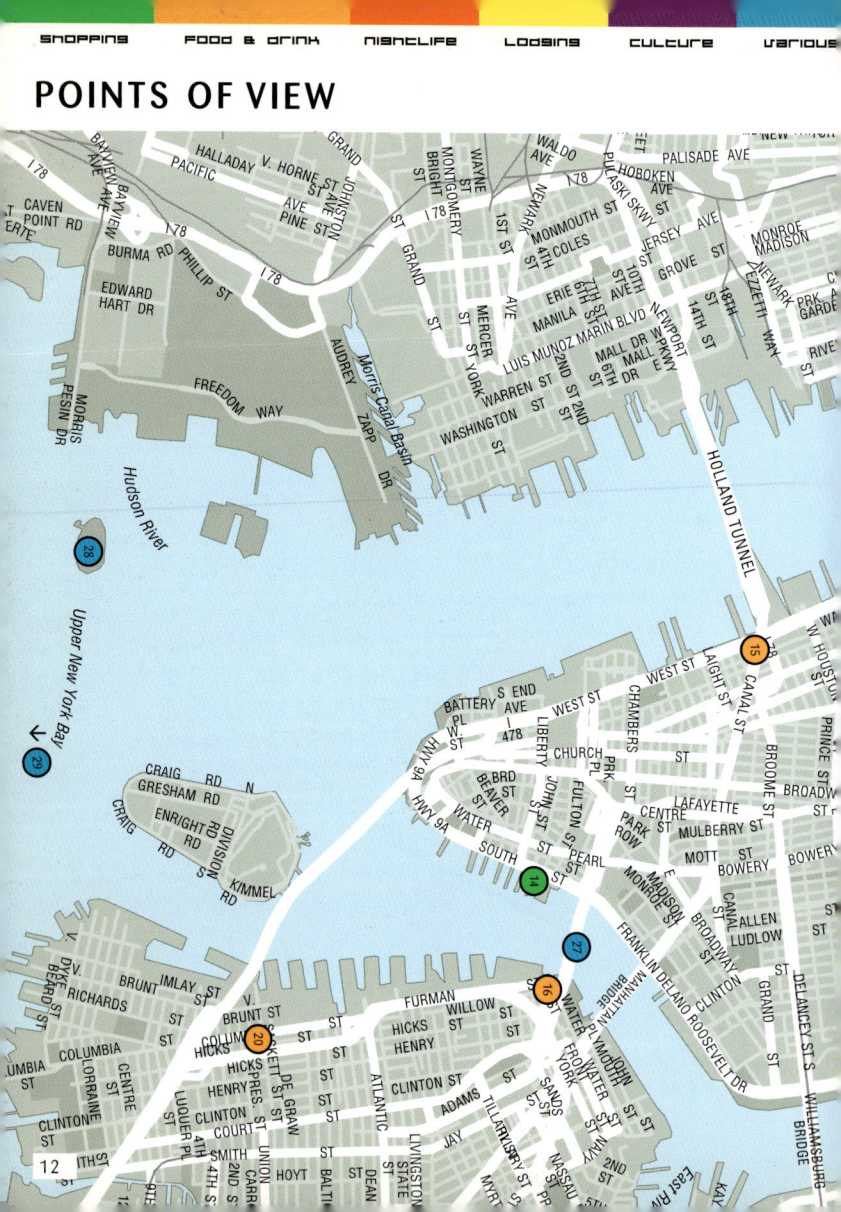

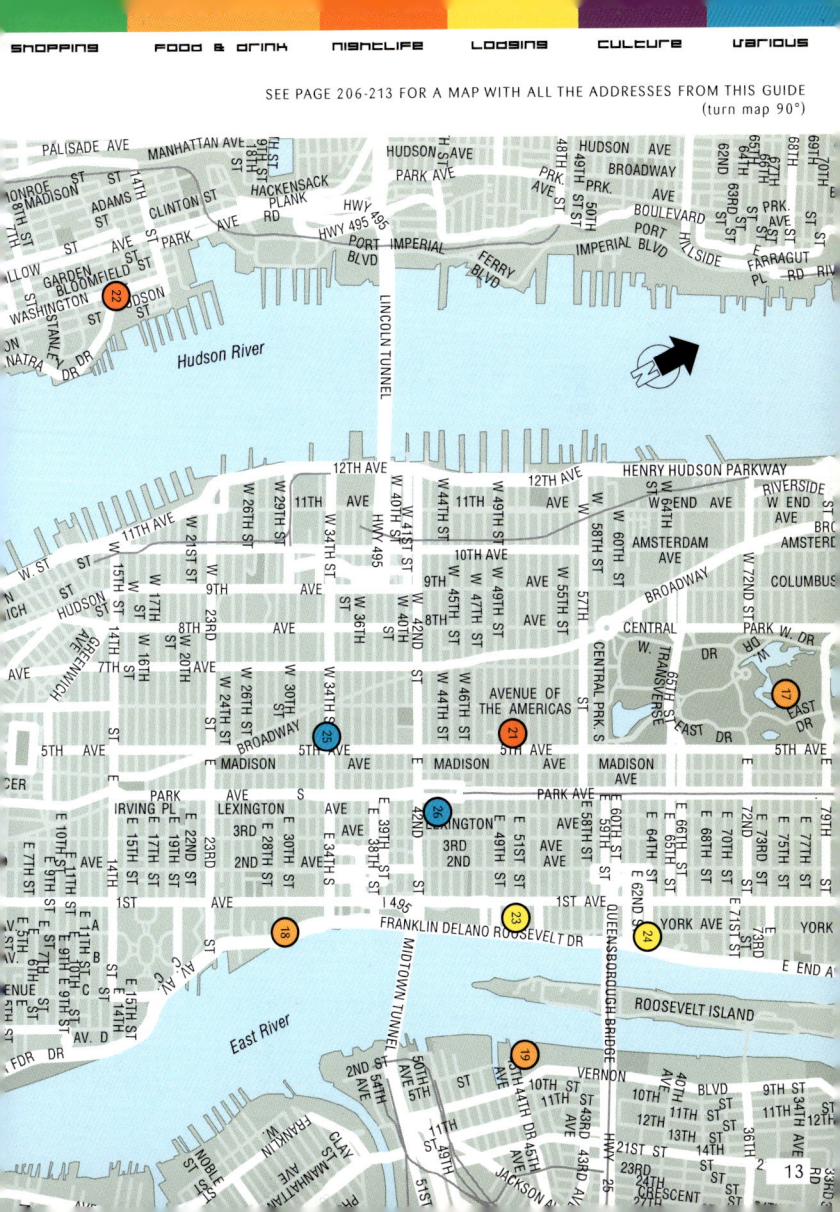

SEE PAGE 206-213 FOR A MAP WITH ALL THE ADDRESSES FROM THIS GUIDE
(turn map 90°)

ADDRESS 19 fulton street, at east river **TELEPHONE** 212 732 7678 **OPENING HOURS** 10am-7pm, restaurant hours vary **SUBWAY** 2, 3, 4, 5, j, m, z to fulton street, a, c to broadway/nassau

SOUTH STREET SEAPORT number 14, map F

South Street Seaport may seem like thousands of malls across America from the inside, but how many other malls can attest to this much history? This mall is housed at the end of a cobblestone pier dating back to the 1600s. Enjoy a meal, a drink or a free concert in the outdoor plaza, and explore the interesting maritime museum or still-operating Fulton Fish market. If this isn't enough to satisfy you, how about pulling up a chair or grabbing a spot on the steps to stare at the outstanding view of the Brooklyn and Manhattan bridges for a little while? The best thing about this part... It's free!

shopping food & drink nightlife lodging culture various

How do you make a lobster angry? (We've heard it has something to do with hot peppers and oil.) You can ask one of the kitchen staff at F. Illi Ponte, but there's no guarantee they'll give away the secret to one of their most popular dishes. This Tribeca Italian restaurant, located in what was once a longshoremen's hotel, serves up authentic pasta and meat dishes and an excellent selection of wines. It is most notable, however, for its intriguing interior – filled with archways, beams and bricks – and its incredible views across the Hudson River to New Jersey. Try to get a table next to one of the 16-foot windows.

number 15, map E **F. ILLI PONTE**

ADDRESS 39 desbrosses street, at west street **TELEPHONE** 212 226 4621 **WEBSITE** www.filliponte.com
OPENING HOURS mon-thu 11.30am-3.30pm, 5.30-10.30pm, fri 11.30am-3.30pm, 5.30-11.30pm, sat 5.30-11.30pm **CREDIT CARDS** visa, mastercard, amex, diners club **PRICE** $28 **SUBWAY** 1, 9 to canal street

shopping   food & drink   nightlife   lodging   culture   various

It's hard to decide whether the food or the view takes the starring role at this high-end eatery. Several of the nation's most notable chefs had their start at this floating restaurant nestled snugly at the foot of the Brooklyn Bridge. Your view of the lower tip of Manhattan will make the trip to Brooklyn worth the effort – this is undeniably one of the most romantic spots in New York. Try entrees such as venison loin or grilled Mediterranean sea bass, or treat yourself to the chef's signature tasting menu. Either way, you won't soon forget this dining experience. This is considered one of the best restaurants in the world.

ADDRESS 1 water street, at old fulton street, brooklyn **TELEPHONE** 718 522 5200
WEBSITE www.therivercafe.com **OPENING HOURS** (lunch) mon-sat noon-3pm, (dinner) mon-sun 6-11pm, (brunch) sun 11am-3pm **CREDIT CARDS** visa, mastercard, amex, diners club, discover **PRICE** (lunch) $25 (dinner) prix fixe $72 (brunch) $35 **SUBWAY** 2, 3 to clark street, a, c to high street/brooklyn bridge

RIVER CAFÉ   number 16, map F

shopping　　food & drink　　nightlife　　lodging　　culture　　various

THE BOAT HOUSE IN CENTRAL PARK

number 17, map C

ADDRESS central park lake, park drive north at 72nd street **TELEPHONE** 212 517 2233 **WEBSITE** www.thecentralparkboathouse.com **OPENING HOURS** (lunch year-round) daily noon-4pm (dinner mar-oct) daily 5-10pm (brunch year-round) sat-sun 11am-3.30pm **CREDIT CARDS** visa, mastercard, amex, diners club **PRICE** $30 **SUBWAY** 6 to 68th street/hunter college, b, c to 72nd street

Make your reservation well in advance to enjoy sitting right beside the lake at this restaurant in the middle of Central Park. The other dining option inside the park is Tavern on the Green, but the Boat House is more serene and graceful and has a far better view. Menus are seasonal and highlight seafood dishes and fresh ingredients. Surrounded by trees, water and an unobstructed horizon, you might imagine that you've taken a trip to a country manor. However, you'll definitely remember you're in New York when you witness spirited young revelers competing fiercely for a waterfront seat at the adjacent bar.

shopping　　　food & drink　　　nightlife　　　lodging　　　culture　　　various

ADDRESS 500 east 30th street, at FDR drive **TELEPHONE** 212 683 3333 **WEBSITE** www.thewaterclub.com
OPENING HOURS (lunch) daily noon-2.30pm (dinner) daily 5.45-10pm, reservations and jackets required
(brunch) sun 11am-2.30pm **CREDIT CARDS** visa, mastercard, amex, diners club, discover **PRICE** $29
SUBWAY 6 to 28th street

THE WATER CLUB number 18, map D

Blue blazers with gold buttons and crisply parted hair are the uniform of the Water Club's regular patrons. The seafood menu and location on the East River further enhance the yacht club ambiance. Only in such a stately restaurant would patrons hardly blink at paying nearly $100 for a perfectly succulent lobster shelled for you at the table. Try a dry aged sirloin steak or rack of lamb if you don't fancy seafood. The upstairs Crow's Nest, a seasonal outdoor patio with a more moderately priced menu, is open from mid-May through late September and offers an equally great view of the river.

shopping | food & drink | nightlife | lodging | culture | various

Dining by the water in New York generally means making advance reservations, dressing up and having formal meals, and Water's Edge is no exception. Every table at this Queens restaurant has a view, and the free ferry ride for dinner reservations is like a mini-vacation itself. The prix fixe menu prominently features fish and other sea creatures and offers enough choice to keep things interesting. Start with selections like raw oysters or scallops Provencal, and then move on to entrees such as seared king salmon or Atlantic halibut. Reservations and jackets are required. Try to come for dinner, when the view of the city's sparkling nighttime skyline is spectacular.

number 19, map D WATER'S EDGE

ADDRESS 44th drive, at vernon boulevard, long island city, queens **TELEPHONE** 718 482 0033
WEBSITE www.watersedgenyc.com **OPENING HOURS** (lunch) mon-fri noon-3pm (dinner) mon-sat 6-11pm
CREDIT CARDS visa, mastercard, amex, diners club, discover **PRICE** tasting menus from $55
SUBWAY e, v to 23rd street/ely avenue, free ferry service available

shopping   Food & drink   nightlife   Lodging   culture   various

Natural light pours through the windows of this three-story Mexican restaurant, beautifully highlighting the citrus-colored walls, Mexican folk art and exposed brick. Alma means "soul" in Spanish, and this place has got plenty of it. The bar on the ground floor attracts a loyal crowd of locals, while the windows in the upstairs restaurant and the top-level roof deck offer Manhattan skyline views off in the distance. Deliciously fresh Mexican food and zesty drinks will ensure you won't want to roam too far. Expect a crowd on weekends.

ADDRESS 187 columbia street, at degraw street, carroll gardens, brooklyn **TELEPHONE** 718 643 5400 **WEBSITE** www.almarestaurant.com **OPENING HOURS** restaurant (brunch) sat-sun 10am-2.30pm, (dinner) sun-thu 5.30-10pm, fri-sat 5.30-11pm, bar daily 1pm-4am **CREDIT CARDS** visa, mastercard, amex **PRICE** $14 **SUBWAY** f, g to bergen street

ALMA   number 20, map F

shopping | food & drink | nightlife | lodging | culture | various

RAINBOW ROOM

number 21, map C

ADDRESS 30 rockefeller center, between 49th and 50th streets **TELEPHONE** 212 632 5000 **OPENING HOURS** fri 7pm-1am **CREDIT CARDS** visa, mastercard, amex, diners club, discover **PRICE** prix fixe $150 **SUBWAY** b, d, f, v to 47th/50th streets/rockefeller center

Slip on your tuxedo, dark suit or slinky ball gown and head to the 65th floor of Rockefeller Center for a night you won't soon forget. From the time it was built in the 1930s, the Rainbow Room has symbolized glamour, elegance and luxury. The ballroom, with its revolving dance floor, seems something out of an Art Deco fairy tale and offers sweeping views over Manhattan in three directions. On Friday evenings, $150 gets you a special three-course dinner, a big band orchestra and a fabulous night of dancing. Over the years, entertainers such as Tommy Dorsey, Guy Lombardo, Tony Bennett and Louis Armstrong have performed here.

ADDRESS 1039 washington street, at 11th street, hoboken, new jersey **TELEPHONE** 201 653 1703 **WEBSITE** www.maxwellsnj.com **OPENING HOURS** (club) tue-thu 4pm-2am, fri-sat 4pm-3am, sun 11-2am (dinner) sun-thu 5pm-midnight fri-sat 5pm-1am (brunch) sun 11.30am-4pm **PRICE** average drink $6 **SUBWAY** Port Authority Trans-Hudson (PATH) train to Hoboken, then cab, bus or walk

MAXWELL'S number 22, map C

Maxwell's is considered one of the best venues for live music in New York (even though it's really in New Jersey). New Yorkers love to malign their neighboring state whenever possible, but they make exceptions for things like this well-known bar that has helped launch the careers of many an indie rock band. Inside, the room is small and provides an intimate performance space with an excellent sound system. There's a good selection of beer and pub food, and – best of all – one block away is a breathtaking view of Manhattan. It takes a bit of effort to get out to Maxwell's, but it's worth the ride across the river.

shopping   food & drink   nightlife   lodging   culture   various

Visiting diplomats and dignitaries favor the Beekman for its proximity to the United Nations and because every room is a spacious suite, fully equipped with a kitchen and sitting area. The tower, built in 1928, is a designated landmark and a shining example of Art Deco design. Rooms are plush and comfortable and suited to long-term stays, with concierge, valet, laundry and grocery shopping services. Top of the Tower, the urbane restaurant and lounge on the 26th floor, is open daily for dinner and offers an impressive panorama of the city by night, while the Zephyr Grill serves three meals a day in lavish surroundings. Prepare to be pampered.

number 23, map D   **BEEKMAN TOWER HOTEL**

ADDRESS 3 mitchell place, 49th street at 1st avenue **TELEPHONE** 212 355 7300 **WEBSITE** www.affinia.com
PRICE from $160 **CREDIT CARDS** (top of the tower) visa, mastercard, amex, discover
SUBWAY 6, e, v to 51st street

shopping   food & drink   nightlife   lodging   culture   various

The Bentley is one of New York's most underrated hotels. The modern and plush interior, cool lighting, modern furnishings and marble floors should be enough to make this an instant favorite, but this budget hotel goes a step further by offering fabulous views of the East River and Queensborough Bridge. Upstairs, a restaurant serves breakfast and dinner, and a cappuccino bar provides a caffeine fix 24 hours a day. It's hard to believe this kind of style and such a great location (steps from the best of Upper East Side shops and restaurants) can be this affordable! You can thank me later.

ADDRESS 500 east 62nd street, at york avenue **TELEPHONE** 212 644 6000 **WEBSITE** www.nychotels.com
PRICE from $130, including breakfast **SUBWAY** 4, 5, 6, f, n, r, w to 59th street/lexington avenue

BENTLEY HOTEL   number 24, map D

shopping   food & drink   nightlife   lodging   culture   various

EMPIRE STATE BUILDING
number 25, map C

ADDRESS 350 5th avenue, at 34th street **TELEPHONE** 212 736 3100 **WEBSITE** www.esbnyc.com **OPENING HOURS** daily 9.30am-midnight **PRICE** $11 **SUBWAY** 6 to 33rd street, 1, 2, 3, 9 to 34th street/penn station, b, d, f, n, q, r to 34th street/herald square

This legendary landmark is immediately associated with New York. The pencil-shaped Empire State Building is the result of a competition between the chairmen of General Motors and Chrysler to see who could build the world's tallest building. The Chrysler Building finished first, but the Empire State, which opened in 1931, soon claimed the title and held it for 42 years – until the World Trade Center was built. With the Twin Towers gone, the Empire State's observation deck remains unrivalled as the best place for a bird's-eye view of the city. Pick a clear day to head up, and be prepared for windy, sometimes cool conditions and long lines.

ADDRESS 405 lexington avenue, between 42nd and 43rd streets **WEBSITE** www.luciddreams.com/chryslerbuilding **OPENING HOURS** not open to public **SUBWAY** 4, 5, 6, 7, s to 42nd street/grand central

CHRYSLER BUILDING number 26, map D

No other building in New York captures the spirit, elegance and grace of the Art Deco age better than the Chrysler Building. The building is automotive pioneer Walter P. Chrysler's lasting legacy to the city. The soaring tower was – for a short time anyway – the tallest building in the world, and its steel spire is one of the most beautiful and unmistakable sights on the New York skyline. The upper floors house offices, which are no longer open to the public, but the lobby is worth a visit to see the colorful mural and steel and marble details.

shopping   food & drink   nightlife   lodging   culture   various

More than 2500 pedestrians cross the Brooklyn Bridge every day; you should join them. The bridge's Gothic archways are beautiful in their own right, and the bustling activity of cars, bikes, pedestrians and subway trains is exhilarating. Try heading from Manhattan to Brooklyn just before sunset so you can catch the colors of the sky as the sun dips behind the buildings (although you'll have to make frequent stops to turn around). On the other side, you can grab some dinner and then take a stroll along the Brooklyn Heights Promenade for more great views of Manhattan and the Statue of Liberty.

number 27, map F **BROOKLYN BRIDGE**

ADDRESS spans from manhattan's park row to brooklyn's cadman plaza **SUBWA**Y 6 to brooklyn bridge/city hall, a, c to high street

Lady Liberty still greets visitors to New York harbor as she has done since 1886, when France gifted her to the United States. It's again possible to go inside the statue, although it was closed for three years due to security concerns following September 11th, 2001. For those not in any shape to climb the stairs, the island provides excellent views of the city as well as an opportunity to view the statue from the ground up and read the famous inscription. But if you can make it to the top, the view is worth the climb.

ADDRESS liberty island, new york harbor **TELEPHONE** 212 363 3200 **WEBSITE** www.nps.gov/stli **OPENING HOURS** daily 9.30am-5pm **PRICE** $10 round-trip ferry fee (includes a stop at Ellis Island) **SUBWAY** 1, 9 to south ferry, 4, 5 to bowling green, n, r to whitehall street, then take ferry

STATUE OF LIBERTY number 28, map E

shopping   food & drink   nightlife   lodging   culture   various

number 29, map E   GREAT KILLS PARK

ADDRESS hylan boulevard, staten island **TELEPHONE** 718 987 6790 **OPENING HOURS** daily sunrise to sunset, extended summer hours, permits available for certain after-hours activities **PRICE** free **SUBWAY** 1, 9 to south ferry, then staten island ferry to st. george terminal, take tottenville-bound s78 bus (d ramp) along hylan blvd, get off at great kills park entrance, then walk to crooke's point (two miles)

Some secret hideaways can't stay secret for long. Great Kills Park and Beach is one of them. Only a 30-minute bus ride from the Staten Island Ferry terminal, the park offers a beautiful beach, a marina, hiking trails, playing fields and excellent spots for fishing. During the day you can admire the views of Lower New York Bay from Crooke's Point, and at night you can gaze at the heavens and see more stars than in any other location in New York. Park rangers organize special stargazing events (remember, safety in numbers), so call ahead for schedules and other information.

| shopping | food & drink | nightlife | loosing | culture | various |

NYC 24/7

FROM SOHA TO BOCOCA

There's a **funny phenomenon** in New York. It's both strange and humorous and can probably only trace its roots back about three or four decades. It seems to happen almost spontaneously, and it goes something like this: An area of the city – an innocent stretch of crisscrossed streets – begins to attract the attention of new residents and storeowners, infusing it with an invigorated sense of character. The area starts to garner attention, and suddenly it's christened with a funny **acronymic name**.

It could be said that it all started with **SoHo**, a contraction that ostensibly stands for "South of Houston," but also calls to mind the infamous Soho area of London, England. In the first half of the 1900s, this area of New York was filled with **slums and sweatshops** and was anything but fashionable. In fact, in those days it was referred to as "Hell's Hundred Acres!" Later, the mostly Italian residents of the area simply referred to it as the "South Village." It was not until the 1950s, when **artists** began to transform **abandoned warehouse lofts** into studio space, that SoHo as we know it today began to take form.

Artists rented huge lofts for just a few hundred dollars a month, often with leases that lasted ten or 20 years. These spaces, though they existed in what was thought of as an industrial wasteland, had **high ceilings, large windows** and plenty of natural light. The artists often had to rig up their own plumbing and live with temperamental heat, rodents and desolate streets at night, but the benefits far outweighed these hardships. Soon **galleries** began to spring up, and before long the area became a bona fide neighborhood and art district.

At the same time, urban planners began to recognize the **small area** south of SoHo that was bounded by Canal Street, Church Street, Park Place and the Hudson River. Originally one of the **oldest sections of New York**, the area had, by the 1960s, become neglected and was dismissed by all commercial enterprise. City planners coined the name **TriBeCa**, a shortened version of "Triangle Below Canal." Soon after that, redevelopment plans were put into place, paving the way for the **high-priced and fashionable** apartments, restaurants and shops that now fill the locality.

In the last few years, New York has seen the birth of **NoHo** (North of Houston), **NoLiTa** (North of Little Italy), **SoHa** (South of Harlem), as well as Brooklyn's **DUMBO** (Down Under Manhattan Bridge Overpass) and **BoCoCa** (Boerum Hill, Cobble Hill and Carroll Gardens).

shopping　　　food & drink　　　nightlife　　　lodging　　　culture　　　various

Many New Yorkers now make a **joke** of the nicknaming craze, calling that part of the Upper West Side above 82nd Street **"NoZa"** – North of Zabar's – or dubbing the progressively trendy area in Brooklyn near Morgan and Flushing Avenues **"MoFlo."** These jokesters had better beware, however. As soon as hungry real estate developers pick up on these ironic monikers, there's a good chance the names will be **marketed**, rents will rise and new "neighborhoods" will be born.

Acronyms must be **contagious**, because they're everywhere in New York. They've basically replaced certain words in regular parlance (the city's police force is almost always known as NYPD, and ever since September 11, 2001 ("9/11"), you hear and see FDNY instead of the Fire Department). Acronyms have **invaded** shop and restaurant names too and don't look like they're planning a retreat any time soon. So take the IRT to LES, buy a dress at DKNY, see a show at CBGB, and then **take the PATH** out to JC. All in a day in **NYC!** (Translation for non-New Yorkers: "Take the subway to the Lower East Side, buy a designer dress, attend a concert at a rock club, then travel on the Trans-Hudson train line to Jersey City.")

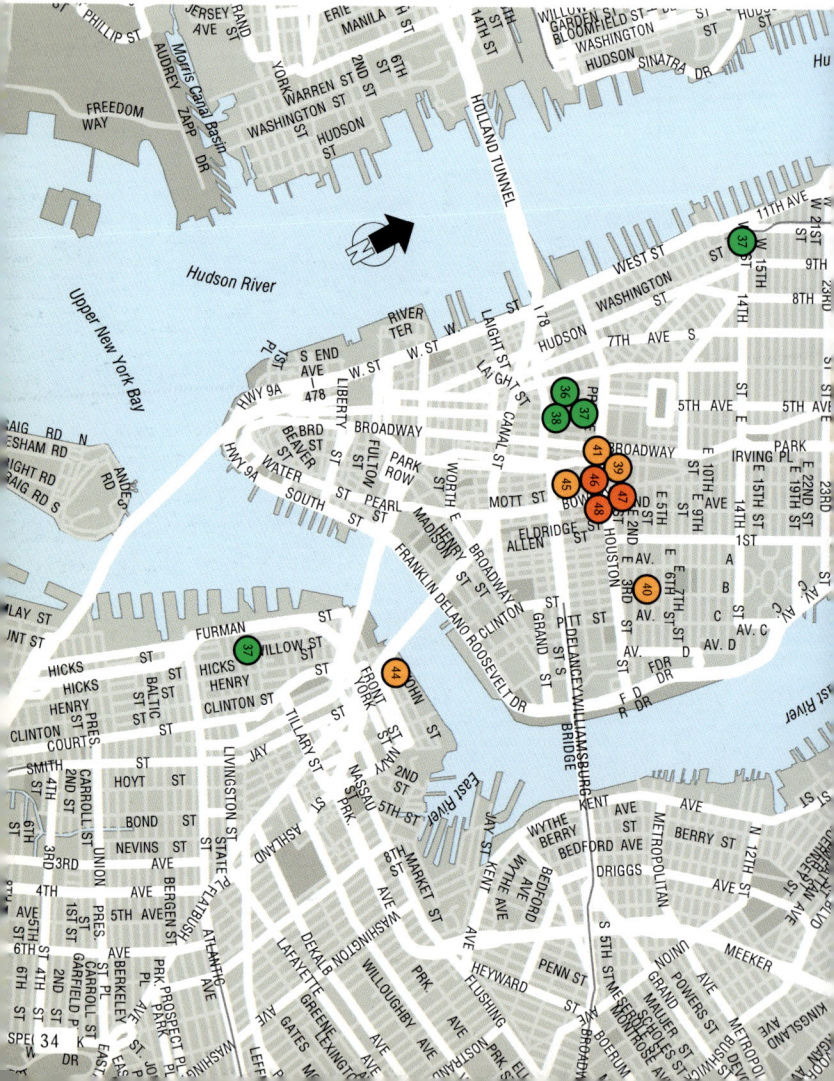

NYC 24/7

34

shoppen | food & drink | nightlife | lodging | culture | various

SEE PAGE 206-213 FOR A MAP WITH ALL THE ADDRESSES FROM THIS GUIDE
(turn map 90°)

35

shopping · food & drink · nightlife · lodging · culture · various

ADDRESS (1) 655 madison avenue, at 60th street (2) 420 west broadway, near prince street **TELEPHONE** (1) 212 223 3569 (2) 646 613 1100 **WEBSITE** www.dkny.com **OPENING HOURS** (1) mon-wed, fri 10am-8pm, thu, sat 10am-9pm, sun 11am-7pm (2) mon-sat 11am-8pm, sun noon-7pm **CREDIT CARDS** visa, mastercard, amex **SUBWAY** (1) n, r to 5th avenue, 4, 5, 6, q to 59th street (2) c, e to spring street

DKNY number 36, map C, E

Raised in Long Island and educated at New York's Parsons School of Design, Donna Karan has become one of the world's most recognizable designer names. Her aesthetic epitomizes New York style – urban and sophisticated, yet simple and comfortable. The two Manhattan DKNY "lifestyle" boutiques feature her street-wise collection of clothes for men and women, as well as a wide range of other products. Browse the feng shui-like, brightly lit environments, and you will soon long for this lifestyle yourself. From vintage clothing to coffee table books, shoes, clothes, home furnishings, fragrances and even an organic café, Donna's got you covered, both inside and out!

shopping   food & drink   nightlife   lodging   culture   various

DWR provides easy access to the kind of well-designed furniture that was previously only available in high-end interior design showrooms. Each design studio (there are three in New York) is carefully chosen for its own architectural merit and then methodically designed in order to best display the furniture. Pieces include designs by the legendary Ray and Charles Eames, Mies van der Rohe and Alvar Aalto, as well as the work of younger designers such as Philippe Starck and Ron Arad and some pieces exclusive to DWR. Even if you don't buy anything, walking through one of these beautifully appointed stores is like visiting a modern design museum.

number 37, map C, E, F **DWR (DESIGN WITHIN REACH)**

ADDRESS (1) 408 west 14th street, between 9th and 10th avenues (2) 142 wooster street, between prince and houston streets (3) 76 montague street, brooklyn heights **TELEPHONE** (1) 212 242 9449 (2) 212 475 0001 (3) 718 643 1015 **WEBSITE** www.dwr.com **OPENING HOURS** (all locations) mon-sat 11am-7pm, sun noon-6pm **CREDIT CARDS** visa, mastercard, amex **SUBWAY** (1) a, c, e, l to 14th street/8th avenue (2) n, r to prince street (3) 2, 3 to clark street

shopping   food & drink   nightlife   lodging   culture   various

SoHo is all about shopping, and shopping is all about enjoyment at this boutique. This is an extremely welcoming environment, with hip music, playful clothing, flattering lighting and friendly staff. A sign by the door invites you to "come in, hang out and make yourself at home" and promises that you'll leave looking lovely. The store prides itself on carrying hard-to-find designers like Alice Roi, Martine Sitbon and Behnaz Sarafpour, but it's not hard to find Kirna Zabete: Smart shoppers will be magnetically drawn to it. If your wardrobe is crying out for an infusion of super-hip, you'll find everything you're looking for at this self-described "style supermarket."

ADDRESS 96 greene street, between prince and spring streets **TELEPHONE** 212 941 9656
WEBSITE www.kirnazabete.com **OPENING HOURS** mon-sat 11am-7pm, sun noon-6pm **CREDIT CARDS** visa, mastercard, amex **SUBWAY** n, r to prince street

KIRNA ZABETE   number 38, map E

number 39, map F B-BAR & GRILL

ADDRESS 40 east 4th street, at bowery **TELEPHONE** 212 475 2220 **WEBSITE** www.bbarandgrill.com **OPENING HOURS** mon 11.30am-midnight, tue-fri 11.30-1am, sat 10.30-1am, sun 10.30am-midnight **CREDIT CARDS** visa, mastercard, amex, diners club **PRICE** $17 **SUBWAY** 6 to bleecker street, f, s, v to broadway/lafayette street

This restaurant/bar/club is many things to many people. It was once the epitome of celebrity cool and before that was home to a gas station catering mostly to cab drivers. The cabbies and A-listers have now moved on, but the crowds keep packing into B-Bar. The outdoor patio is particularly popular in warm weather, but the cozy indoor booths and lounge-y sofas are filled in any weather. Where else but in NoHo, the cutesy name for the otherwise non-descript area north of Houston Street and east of Broadway, could a restaurateur dream of finding nearly 6500 square feet of space?

ADDRESS (1) 41 avenue b, between 3rd and 4th streets (2) 1626 2nd avenue, between 84th and 85th streets **TELEPHONE** (1) 212 477 1021 (2) 212 327 1327 **WEBSITE** www.dtut.com **OPENING HOURS** (1) daily 8am-midnight (2) sun-thu 8am-midnight, fri-sat 8-2am **CREDIT CARDS** visa, mastercard, amex **PRICE** $7 **SUBWAY** (1) f, v to lower east side/2nd avenue (2) 4, 5, 6 to 86th street

DT/UT number 40, map B, F

These two cozy, comfortable café/lounges suffer from an identity crisis. They are not sure if they are downtown hipster-cool or uptown family-friendly, so they've decided to split the difference. The result: DT/UT, which stands for downtown/uptown. Both locations are ideally situated in their respective neighborhoods (Alphabet City and the Upper East Side), and both feature galleries, live music and children's story time. The food menus offer a wide variety of typical café fare – from Belgian waffles to brownies, cakes and pies, sandwiches, soups, quiches and fondues. There is also a beer and wine list and even a happy hour at the downtown location.

shopping   food & drink   nightlife   lodging   culture   various

Whatever your pleasure, you'll find it at this enigmatic restaurant slightly off the beaten track. Although it might not be the current in-spot, this place has what many trendy restaurateurs would kill for – longevity. It's been serving up consistently good food for nearly two decades. NoHo Star is perfect for a morning pick-me-up, lunchtime pasta or prime rib dinner and also offers an excellent Chinese menu in the evenings. The dessert menu is available for those who want to stop in after dining or drinking somewhere else and there's a selection of weekly dinner and dessert specials as well. Ed Koch ate breakfast here every day while he was mayor.

number 41, map E **NOHO STAR**

ADDRESS 330 lafayette street, at bleecker street **TELEPHONE** 212 925 0070 **WEBSITE** www.nohostar.com
OPENING HOURS mon-fri 8am-midnight, sat-sun 10.30am-midnight **CREDIT CARDS** visa, mastercard, amex, diners club, discover **PRICE** $16 **SUBWAY** 6 to bleecker street, f, s, v to broadway/lafayette street

The smell of perfectly cooked rice is the first thing that hits you as you enter this tiny, minimalist, midtown lunch spot. Oms/b is Japanese shorthand for "omusubi," stuffed or wrapped rice balls that are served everywhere in Japan. Sushi rice is shaped into bite-sized spheres, pucks or triangles and then filled or covered with traditional Japanese ingredients like fried cod roe, Japanese plum or spicy tuna. At Oms/b, New Yorkers can also have their "omusubi" topped with more familiar foods, like prosciutto, pastrami or tuna with mayonnaise. The space is small and sparse, with white tiles and polished wooden tables, and prices are low enough to make this a daily stop.

ADDRESS 156 east 45th street, between 3rd and lexington avenues **TELEPHONE** 212 922 9788
OPENING HOURS mon-fri 8am-7pm, sat 10am-7pm **CREDIT CARDS** none **PRICE** $2 **SUBWAY** 4, 5, 6, 7, s to 42nd street/grand central

OMS/B number 42, map D

number 43, map D **212**

ADDRESS 133 east 65th street, between park and lexington avenues **TELEPHONE** 212 249 6565 **WEBSITE** www.212restaurant.com **OPENING HOURS** sun-wed noon-midnight, thu-sat noon-1am **CREDIT CARDS** visa, mastercard, amex **PRICE** $18 **SUBWAY** 6 to 68th street/hunter college

The number 212 is characteristic of life in Manhattan. Until recently, 212 was the only telephone area code assigned to Manhattan addresses; the outer boroughs had 718, which was considered far inferior. Things have changed (now Manhattan has 917 and 646), but the 212 legend lives on at this sensual Upper East Side bar and restaurant. The menu features creative dishes such as pan-seared red snapper and Maine lobster club sandwich, as well as a delectable array of desserts. Head down to the dark, sexy bar for your choice of 75 vodkas from around the world, an extensive wine list and an assortment of specialty drinks, including White Chocolate Martini.

ADDRESS 126 front street, at pearl street, dumbo **TELEPHONE** 718 243 9005 **OPENING HOURS** (lunch) wed-fri 11am-3pm (dinner) tue-sat 6-11pm sun 6-10pm (brunch) sun 11am-3pm **CREDIT CARDS** visa, mastercard, amex **PRICE** $15 **SUBWAY** a, c to high street, f to york street

SUPERFINE number 44, map F

Dumbo is the kind of place where an old auto parts warehouse makes the perfect location for a bar and grill. Superfine embodies the essence of the neighborhood – cool, casual and non-conformist. Local artists display their work and play pool while diners cram in for lunch, dinner or brunch on Sundays. The menu offers up a daily selection of Mediterranean-inspired dishes, made from ingredients freshly-picked that day at the local farmer's market. You never know what might be featured on the chalkboard menu, but it is sure to include vegetarian options, salads that are full meals and fresh fish. This restaurant is truly a labor of love, and it shows.

shopping   food & drink   nightlife   lodging   culture   various

This tiny bistro is best in warm weather when, after a long day spent strolling the streets of NoLiTa, you can kick back in the pebbled backyard, put your feet up and enjoy a beer or wine "al fresco." Service is always friendly and upbeat, and the menu – with selections such as "coq au vin" and "tarte tatin" – is very French. Margot is particularly popular on Sundays for brunch – imagine whiling away a few hours as you sip "café au lait," nibble on a delicious omelet and contemplate your day's plan. It's as though you've been transported to romantic Paris without ever leaving your table.

number 45, map E # BISTROT MARGOT

ADDRESS 26 prince street, between elizabeth and mott streets **TELEPHONE** 212 274 1027 **OPENING HOURS** sun-thu 11am-11pm, fri-sat 11am-midnight **CREDIT CARDS** none **PRICE** $15 **SUBWAY** 6 to spring street, n, r, w to prince street

CBGB was once considered hallowed ground for cutting-edge underground music, and although these days it looks like an aging rock star itself, for many coming here is a like a pilgrimage. It's a bit sleazy, not particularly clean and has one of the most notorious washrooms in the city, but this is where underground bands like the Ramones, Blondie and the Talking Heads got their start in the 1970s, and even today you can catch some aggressively independent music. The hard-to-pronounce initials stand for "Country Bluegrass Blues and Other Music for Uplifting Gormandizers," which is what the bar's owner originally intended to showcase. It's a good thing that didn't happen.

ADDRESS 315 bowery, at bleecker street **TELEPHONE** 212 982 4052 **WEBSITE** www.cbgb.com **OPENING HOURS** sun 3pm-1am, mon-thu 7pm-3am, fri-sat 8pm-4am **CREDIT CARDS** none **SUBWAY** 6 to bleecker street

CBGB-OMFUG number 46, map F

shopping   food & drink   nightlife   lodging   culture   various

number 47, map F # KGB

ADDRESS 85 east 4th street **TELEPHONE** 212 505 3360 **WEBSITE** www.kgbbar.com **OPENING HOURS** daily 7pm-4am **CREDIT CARDS** none **SUBWAY** 6 to bleecker street, f to second avenue

Although KGB officially stands for Kraine Gallery Bar (a reference to the Kraine Theater downstairs), you'd be forgiven for thinking it an allusion to the former Soviet intelligence agency. This second-floor location once housed the New York headquarters of the Ukrainian Communist Party, and the bar's décor has taken its cues from that legacy. The lighting scheme is red, period posters and portraits of party leaders cover the walls, and dozens of vodkas line the bar. Literary types of all political persuasions frequently drop by for a drink and a reading, and you can always enjoy a night of rowdy conversation with friends, both old and new.

ADDRESS 41 1st avenue, between 2nd and 3rd streets **TELEPHONE** 212 475 5097 **WEBSITE** www.drinkgoodstuff.com
OPENING HOURS daily 1pm-4am **PRICE** $6 **SUBWAY** f, v to lower east side/second avenue

DBA number 48, map F

The mystery behind the name of this East Village bar keeps drinkers guessing night after night. Could it be the Downtown Beverage Association? An encouragement to Drink Beer Anytime? If you can't figure it out, Don't Be Annoyed. Just have a drink, and your worries will disappear. Choices include over 100 beers from around the world, dozens of single malt Scotches, tequila, rum, wine and even hand-drawn cask ales for the real "cognoscenti." The emphasis is on quality, not only in the selection, but also in the storing and serving of these beverages. Ask your bartender for a recommendation if you're truly stumped.

shopping   food & drink   nightlife   lodging   culture   various

While Manhattan's Museum of Modern Art gets a facelift, the institution has moved its exhibition programs to a former Swingline Staple factory in Queens. Better known as MoMA QNS, the redesigned industrial space houses a selection of paintings, photographs and sculptures from the museum's collection and also mounts major traveling exhibitions. MoMA Manhattan is due to open again in 2005 (51st street), but some New Yorkers will miss the openness and gritty character of QNS when its role as foster parent is done. It's refreshing to get out of Manhattan and see masterworks of art in a less-than-pristine environment. Feels like the kind of atmosphere Picasso might have appreciated.

number 49, map D   **MOMA QNS**

ADDRESS 33rd street at queens boulevard **TELEPHONE** 212 708 9400 **WEBSITE** www.moma.org **OPENING HOURS** mon, thu, sat-sun 10am-5pm, fri 10am-7.45pm, closed tue-wed **PRICE** $12 **SUBWAY** 7 (local) to 33rd street

STAR GAZING

A FIXATION FOR FAME AND FORTUNE

Since New Yorkers think of themselves as living in the **Capital of the World**, it's only natural that they expect the rich and famous to eventually join them in their city. And to be frank, they won't have to wait long. Many celebrities have already taken them up on the offer – at least those who didn't grow up in the city before moving to California to make it big. Hollywood stars, pop idols, authors, athletes and loads of other **famous people** seem to **love New York**. Many celebrities own homes here and show their famous faces at nightclubs, trendy restaurants and SoHo boutiques.

New Yorkers are generally pretty respectful of a **celebrity's privacy**. When they see a star on the street, most New Yorkers will do a subtle double-take and then carry on with their business, proud of their **sharp eye** for a **famous face**, but even prouder of their ability to control the urge to **gawk** or ask for autographs.

Once word gets out that a certain celebrity has been seen at a certain place, however, even **the humblest New Yorker** will find it hard to resist **telling a friend** the news or stopping by for a quick peek themselves. You may hear them making excuses: "No, I just really like the way they mix a martini at that bar," they might say, or, "I'm so addicted to **the watermelon face scrub**, I just have to go down and pick some up," but the ulterior motive is clear – the chance for a brush with stardom. Even if the celebrity isn't there when you are, it's enough to know that they've been there before. New Yorkers love to bask in the knowledge that they buy their organic produce at the same greengrocer as Kate Hudson or that their acupuncturist is the same one that **Yoko Ono** sees. At the **legendary Katz's Deli** on the Lower East Side, you can sit beneath a small hand-written sign proclaiming the seat you're in as the very one where **Bill Clinton** sat when he was President of the United States. It even tells you what he ate that day: "two hot dogs, a pastrami sandwich, fries, diet ginger ale and decaf coffee." Diet ginger ale?!!

Once celebrities discover your favorite local spot, you can be sure it won't **remain a secret** for long. The list of places that have been ruined by **overexposure** is thicker than the Manhattan phone book. But a place that's hot one month can fade from the limelight quicker than a Jennifer Lopez marriage. Celebrity is a fickle creature. If you're intent on **a superstar sighting**, check the Internet. There are dozens of message boards where people post up-to-the-minute celebrity **spottings** and list the cool "hangouts du jour."

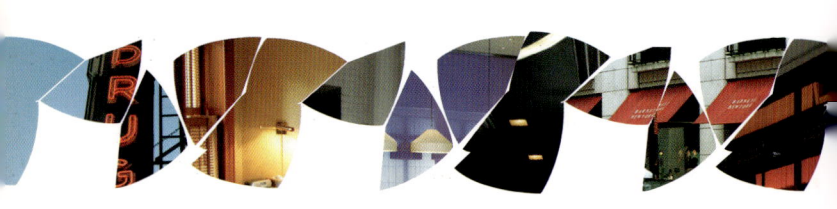

Of course, it's still **hard to predict** where and when you might see a star in New York, but that's part of the fun. It's the difference between going to the zoo and knowing exactly where to find the lions versus going on safari and taking your chances. As with any safari, it's best to **go** directly to the **animal's natural habitat**.

The **West Village and SoHo** remain the **neighborhoods of choice** for most celebrities, along with SoHo's little sisters NoLiTa, NoHo and TriBeCa. Stroll down the streets of these downtown neighborhoods, and you'll have the best chance of bumping into an **A-list star**.

I'll give you some **recommendations** of places to go in this chapter, but I don't want to give away too much information. That would take away from the **thrill of the chase**, now wouldn't it?

STAR GAZING

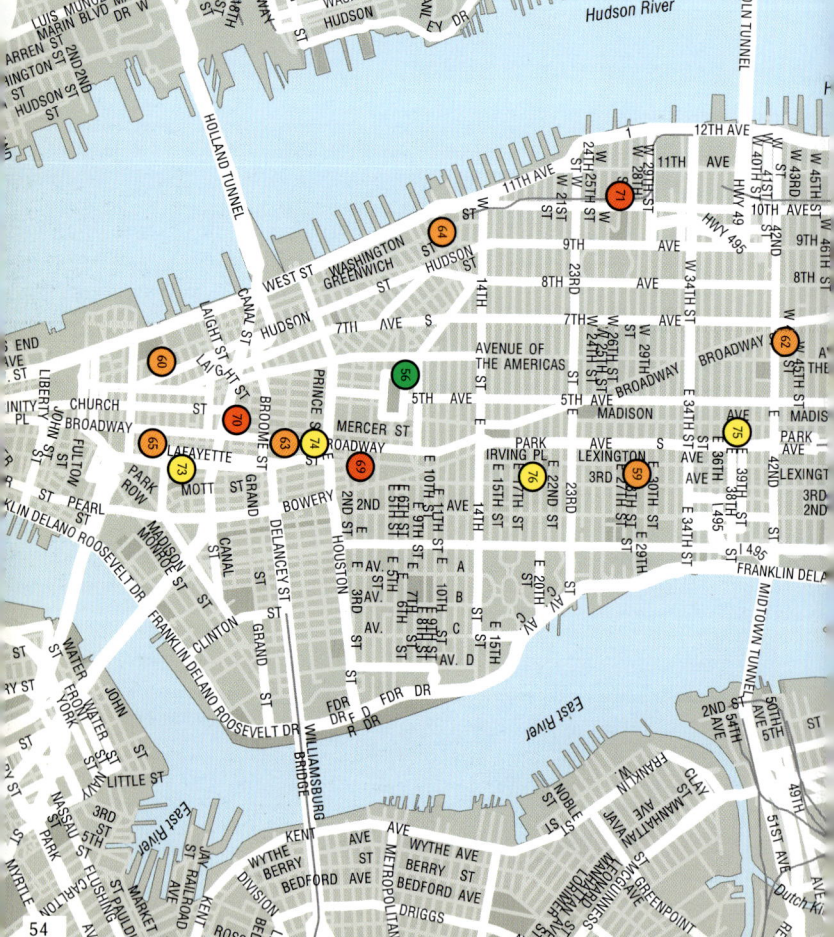

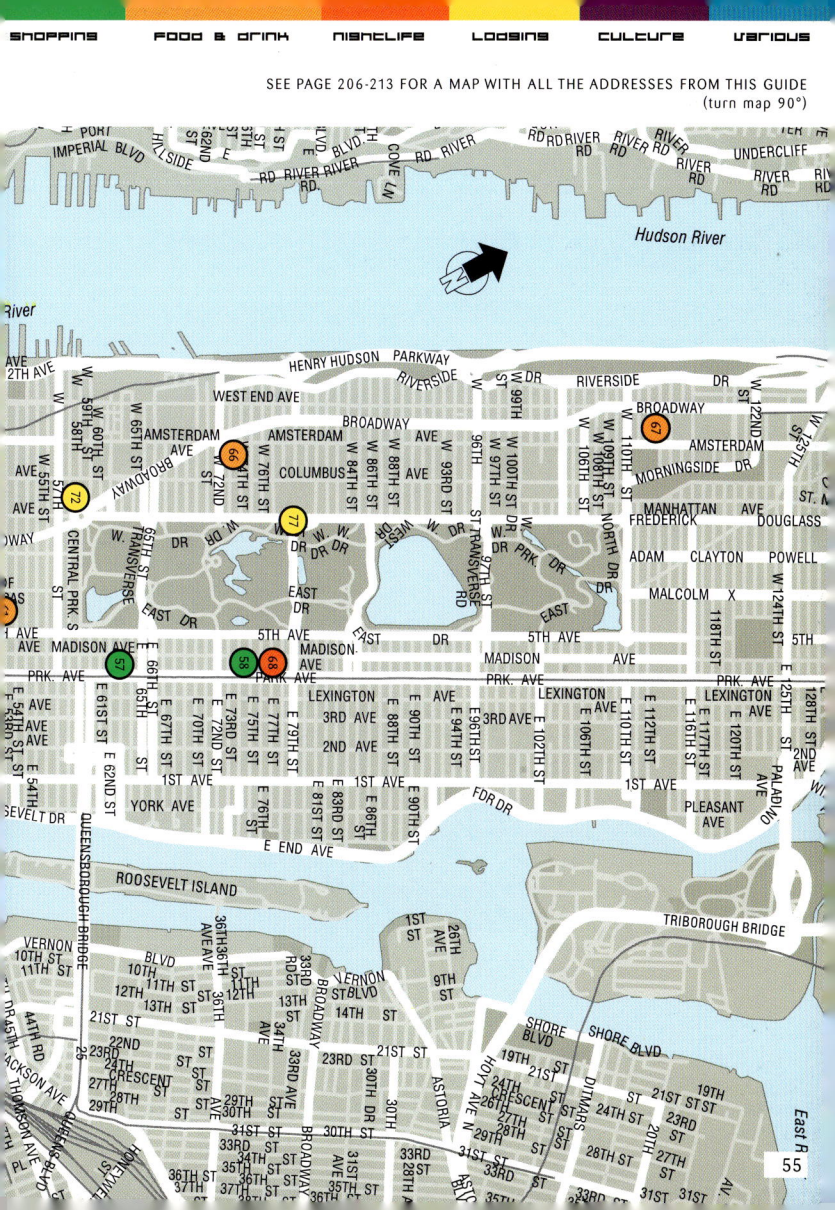

shopping | food & drink | nightlife | lodging | culture | various

SEE PAGE 206-213 FOR A MAP WITH ALL THE ADDRESSES FROM THIS GUIDE
(turn map 90°)

55

ADDRESS 414 sixth avenue, between 8th and 9th streets **TELEPHONE** 212 533 2700 **WEBSITE** www.bigelowchemists.com **OPENING HOURS** mon-fri 7.30am-9pm, sat 8.30am-7pm, sun 8.30am-5.30pm
SUBWAY a, c, e, f, v to west 4th street

C.O. BIGELOW APOTHECARIES
number 56, map E

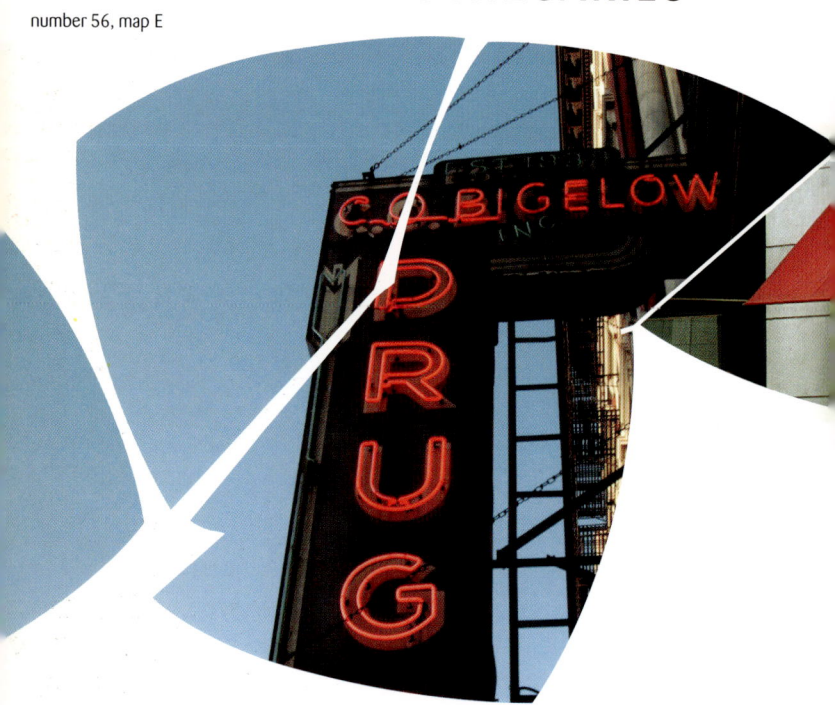

Regular shoppers at this historic pharmacy include supermodel Kate Moss, "Sex and the City" star Sarah Jessica Parker and actresses Susan Sarandon, Holly Hunter and Liv Tyler. The eclectic, international collection of skin and personal care products is impressive, and the store itself – with its wooden shelves and creaky floors – still feels the way it must have when Clarence Otis Bigelow bought it in 1920. Favorite products include Neals Yard Remedies, Dr. Harris shaving creams, Euthymol toothpaste, Philip B's botanical hair products and Bigelow's own line of essential oils. Health nuts will love the excellent selection of homeopathic remedies.

shopping   food & drink   nightlife   lodging   culture   various

At this sleek store for fashionistas, you'll find designs by Prada, Yves Saint Laurent and Marc Jacobs, shoes by Balenciaga and Christian Louboutin and much more. Drop by Fred's on the 9th floor to see what celebrity might be nibbling on a Madison salad. The restaurant is open for lunch, dinner, weekend brunch and high tea on weekdays. Even if you don't see any celebrities, you can act like one by getting the concierge to make you dinner reservations, hail you a cab or book you theater tickets. Then get a personal shopper to pick out the perfect outfit for you. Act the part well enough, and maybe someone will mistake *you* for someone famous!

number 57, map C BARNEYS NEW YORK

ADDRESS 660 madison avenue, between 60th and 61st streets **TELEPHONE** 212 826 8900 **WEBSITE** www.barneys.com **OPENING HOURS** mon-fri 10am-8pm, sat 10am-7pm, sun 11am-6pm **CREDIT CARDS** visa, mastercard, amex, diners club **SUBWAY** n, r, w to 5th avenue

Christian Louboutin is obsessed with shoes, and celebrities – from Madonna to Princess Caroline of Monaco to the ladies of "Sex and the City" – are obsessed with him. His sexy, whimsical, exotic creations (think brocade, tassels and fur) are found on some of the world's most famous and fashionable feet. If you share his obsession with footwear and are willing to make a serious investment (few shoes are less than $350), you'll love this tiny and intimate Upper East Side boutique.

ADDRESS 941 madison avenue, near 74th street **TELEPHONE** 212 396 1884 **OPENING HOURS** mon-sat 10am-6pm **CREDIT CARDS** visa, mastercard, amex **SUBWAY** 6 to 77th street

CHRISTIAN LOUBOUTIN number 58, map A

shopping   food & drink   nightlife   lodging   culture   various

number 59, map D   # LES HALLES

ADDRESS 411 park avenue south, between 28th and 29th streets **TELEPHONE** 212 679 4111 **WEBSITE** www.leshalles.net **OPENING HOURS** daily noon-midnight **CREDIT CARDS** visa, mastercard, amex, discover **SUBWAY** 6 to 28th street

Les Halles' executive chef, Anthony Bourdain, rocketed to fame when he released "Kitchen Confidential," his tell-all book about the sordid underbelly of the restaurant business. He soon found himself with a Food Network television show and several more book contracts, but what Bourdain and Les Halles do best is food. Simple meals such as "steak frites" are the best bets at this intimate, dimly lit French-style brasserie, which makes you feel like you're in Montmartre instead of Murray Hill.

ADDRESS 375 greenwich street, at franklin street **TELEPHONE** 212 941 3900
WEBSITE www.myriadrestaurantgroup.com **OPENING HOURS** (lunch) mon-fri, sun 11.30am-3pm (dinner) mon-thu 5.30-11.30pm, fri-sat 5.30-11.30pm, sun 5.30-10pm **CREDIT CARDS** visa, mastercard, amex, discover **PRICE** $28 (prix fixe $33) **SUBWAY** 1, 9 to franklin street

TRIBECA GRILL number 60, map E

Robert De Niro, Ed Harris, Sean Penn, Christopher Walken and Lou Diamond Phillips. The list reads like the star-studded cast of a Hollywood blockbuster, but these guys are actually together for a different reason: They're investors in the Tribeca Grill. The restaurant opened in a converted coffee warehouse in 1990, before TriBeCa was the hyped and hip location it is now. The huge space respects the memory of the former industrial setting by leaving ducting and pillars exposed, but the bare brick walls are jazzed up by paintings by Robert De Niro's father. The wine selection is stellar, and the dishes are inventive without being pretentious.

shopping   food & drink   nightlife   lodging   culture   various

In the late 1920s, when booze was banned and the jazz age was swinging, "21" became one of the city's most notorious speakeasies. Although it was raided numerous times, nothing could ever be pinned on the owners because of an ingenious system of hiding the liquor that included pulleys, levers, a secret wine cellar and a hidden door. When prohibition ended, "21" continued to be – and still remains today – a popular place for business tycoons, celebrities and VIPs. Enter through the iron gates and past the dozens of jockey statues, and you'll immediately feel the pulse of power that resonates in these walls.

number 61, map C **"21" CLUB**

ADDRESS 21 west 52nd street, between 5th and 6th avenues **TELEPHONE** 212 582 7200 **WEBSITE** www.21club.com **OPENING HOURS** mon-thu noon-2.30pm, 5.30-10pm, fri noon-2.30pm, 5.30-11pm, sat 5.30-11pm **CREDIT CARDS** visa, mastercard, amex, diners club, discover **PRICE** $40 **SUBWAY** b, d, f to 47th/50th streets/rockefeller center

At this theater district landmark, you'll see hundreds of famous faces every day. Colorful caricatures and sketches of celebrities cover practically every square inch of the walls, and it's great fun checking out who's been honored. A meal here is a throwback to the heyday of the Great White Way (as Broadway was once known), when theater and Hollywood celebrities came to Sardi's to see and be seen. Many celebrities continue the tradition to this day, and the restaurant is packed before the curtains rise at nearby theaters. If you want to be certain of getting a table, make sure to plan ahead.

ADDRESS 234 west 44th street, between broadway and 8th avenue **TELEPHONE** 212 221 8440 **WEBSITE** www.sardis.com **OPENING HOURS** tue-thu 11.30am-11.30pm, fri-sat 5.30pm-midnight, sun 3.30-7.30pm **CREDIT CARDS** visa, mastercard, amex, diners club **PRICE** $26 **SUBWAY** 1, 2, 3, 7, 9, n, q, r, s, w to 42nd street/times square

SARDI'S   number 62, map C

shopping　　　Food & drink　　　nightlife　　　Lodging　　　culture　　　various

BALTHAZAR
number 63, map E

ADDRESS 80 spring street, between broadway and crosby streets **TELEPHONE** 212 965 1414 **OPENING HOURS** mon-wed 7.30-1am, thu 7.30-1.30am, fri-sat 7.30-2am, sun 7.30am-midnight **CREDIT CARDS** visa, mastercard, amex **PRICE** $21 **SUBWAY** 6 to spring street, n, r, w to prince street

Balthazar has tremendous staying power, an extremely rare commodity in a world of two-minute trends and fleeting fads. Fashionable, stylish people (famous and non-famous) have been coming to Balthazar for years and still haven't had enough of the ambiance or the French brasserie fare. It's big enough that you don't feel closed in, but small enough to still feel intimate; chic enough to make you feel a part of the scene, but not so exclusive that it makes you feel unwelcome. You may have to come very early to get a table, especially for weekend brunch, but it's worth the wait.

ADDRESS 9 9th avenue, at little west 12th street **TELEPHONE** 212 929 4844 **WEBSITE** www.pastisny.com **OPENING HOURS** sun-thu 9-2am, fri-sat 9-2.30am **PRICE** $20 **CREDIT CARDS** visa, mastercard, amex, diners club **SUBWAY** a, c, e to 14th street, l to 8th avenue

PASTIS number 64, map E

The casual and very hip ambiance of Pastis makes it a swank favorite for breakfast, lunch, dinner, cocktails and late-night snacks. The French bistro décor is perfect, right down to the mirrors on the walls and mosaic tiles on the floor. In fact, owner Keith McNally flew all the furnishings in from Europe to ensure total authenticity. The outdoor café is lovely in good weather, as long as you don't mind the earthy aromas of nearby meatpackers. Opt for hearty bistro fare like "croque monsieur" and "steak frites," wash it down with a glass of namesake "pastis," and soak up the atmosphere of one of New York's most talked-about restaurants.

shopping   Food & drink   nightlife   Lodging   Culture   various

Odeon has been around for 20 or so years, making it a true TriBeCa pioneer. Andy Warhol and other avant-garde artists made regular stops here back in the 1980s – if only the walls could talk! One constant element is the brasserie's menu, which to this day offers up the kind of tasty favorites that have helped put – and keep – Odeon solidly in the hearts of New Yorkers. Friendly service, an upscale-casual atmosphere and good food are this restaurant's hallmarks. Be sure to save room for dessert.

number 65, map E **ODEON**

ADDRESS 145 west broadway, at thomas street **TELEPHONE** 212 233 0507 **OPENING HOURS** mon-thu noon-2am, fri noon-3am, sat 11.30-3am, sun 11.30-2am **PRICE** $18 **CREDIT CARDS** visa, mastercard, amex **SUBWAY** 1, 2, 3, 9, a, c to chambers street

shopping   food & drink   nightlife   lodging   culture   various

This little spot has been featured in so many movies and photo shoots it's a celebrity in its own right. Although the name suggests otherwise, Gray's is more famous for hot dogs than papayas. A popular choice is the "Recession Special," two juicy hot dogs and your choice of fruit drink for less than $3. If you can, grab a spot at the counter, and read some of the entertaining signs hanging around the store. Otherwise, you'll literally be eating on the run, as Gray's has no tables, chairs or other amenities.

ADDRESS 2090 broadway, at 72nd street **OPENING HOURS** daily 24 hours **PRICE** $2 **CREDIT CARDS** none **SUBWAY** 1, 2, 3, 9 to 72nd street

GRAY'S PAPAYA number 66, map C

shopping   food & drink   nightlife   lodging   culture   various

number 67, map A TOM'S RESTAURANT

ADDRESS 2880 broadway, at 112th street **TELEPHONE** 212 864 6137 **OPENING HOURS** thu-sat 24 hours, sun-wed 6-1.30am **PRICE** $8 **CREDIT CARDS** none **SUBWAY** 1, 9 to 110th street/cathedral parkway

Fans of TV's "Seinfeld" will immediately recognize this coffee shop, which served as the exterior shot for the gang's favorite hangout on the show. Although you won't see Jerry and friends here, you might see Kenny Kramer, the man who was the inspiration for the Kramer character, conducting one of his reality tours. With all-night hours on weekends, this diner has long been a popular spot for Columbia University students and other assorted neighborhood characters. Great for basic diner food like grilled cheese sandwiches, omelets, milkshakes and Greek salads. Visitors are advised to stay away from anything too adventurous on the menu.

shopping   food & drink   nightlife   lodging   culture   various

ADDRESS 35 east 76th street, at madison avenue **TELEPHONE** 212 570 7189 **OPENING HOURS** mon-sat 7.30pm–midnight (woody allen performs mondays at 8.45pm) **CREDIT CARDS** visa, mastercard, amex, diners club **PRICE** $75 cover charge **SUBWAY** 6 to 77th street

CAFÉ CARLYLE number 68, map C

On Monday nights, film director Woody Allen plays clarinet with the Eddy Davis New Orleans Jazz Band at this upscale Upper East Side hotel bar and restaurant. It's an elite affair, with a high cover charge, a "jackets required" dress code and a serious ambiance. If you are a fan of jazz and cabaret, of Woody Allen's work or of fine French food, this is a good place to indulge your passions and, of course, a guaranteed celebrity spotting. Reservations are required.

There are no cover charges or guest lists at Joe's Pub for the first two hours of the night, but the velvet rope snaps to attention at 8pm sharp, and guests are either expected to produce a ticket or buy one on the spot. Nightly performances at this sexy jazz club/cabaret are eclectic but of-the-moment, just like the A-list celebrity crowd that attends. Dinner reservations are accepted (and recommended if you want to sit to see the show), but are only held for ten minutes, so be early. Seating after that is very limited. Even if you're standing, you'll be expected to stick to the two-drink-per-person minimum.

number 69, map E # JOE'S PUB

ADDRESS 425 lafayette street, at east 4th street **TELEPHONE** 212 539 8770 **WEBSITE** www.publictheater.org
OPENING HOURS daily 6pm-4am, dinner available till midnight **CREDIT CARDS** visa, mastercard, amex
PRICE cover charge $12-$30, average drink $9 **SUBWAY** 6 to astor place, n, r, w to 8th street

| shopping | food & drink | nightlife | lodging | culture | various |

"SoHo's living room" is how this second-floor bar in the lobby of the Soho Grand Hotel has been described. The hotel and the bar are magnets for media, music, film and fashion types, making the lounge a great place for people watching and celebrity spotting. Gaze out on to SoHo's bustling streets from the floor-to-ceiling windows while you enjoy cutting-edge music, signature cocktails and over-priced appetizers. You'll feel like you're sitting in the pages of "Vogue" magazine.

ADDRESS 310 west broadway, between canal and grand streets **TELEPHONE** 212 965 3000
OPENING HOURS sun-wed noon-1.30am, thu-sat noon-2.30am **CREDIT CARDS** visa, mastercard, amex, discover **PRICE** average drink $12 **SUBWAY** 1, 9, a, c, e to canal street

GRAND BAR AND LOUNGE number 70, map E

number 71, map C # BUNGALOW 8

ADDRESS 515 west 27th street, between 10th and 11th avenues **TELEPHONE** 212 629 3333 **OPENING HOURS** mon-sat 10pm-4am **CREDIT CARDS** visa, mastercard, amex, discover **PRICE** average drink $12 **SUBWAY** c, e to 23rd street

If you can get past the door at this selective bar, you might see Paris Hilton or Leonardo DiCaprio. Even if they're not there, you can at least say you spent the evening at a place where $22 buys a club sandwich and where the staff will arrange for a helicopter to whisk you away. Suffice it to say, you've got to look the part and be prepared to pay for it if you want to mingle with the crowd at this tropical-themed paradise. Come dressed to impress, and don't be dismayed if the doorman won't let you in. The most important thing to remember is: Never let 'em see you sweat!

ADDRESS 356 west 58th street, between 8th & 9th avenues **TELEPHONE** 212 554 6000 **PRICE** from $145
SUBWAY 1, 9, a, b, c, d to 59th st/columbus circle

HUDSON HOTEL number 72, map C

From the moment you enter the door of the Hudson Hotel and travel up the brilliantly colored escalator, you are aware that you're in for a treat. Designed and decorated in a uniquely modern style, the Hudson oozes chic without the attitude. The rooms are small (1000 of them are squeezed in), but comfortable, stylishly decorated and very well priced. If you're lucky enough to score a room facing west, you'll be treated to an excellent view of the Hudson River. The lobby level features two trendy bars, a restaurant and a lovely outdoor terrace.

shopping | food & drink | nightlife | lodging | culture | various

This hotel's contemporary, atrium design allows for a creative lighting setup and creates a conceptual space that's anything but closed in. The focus of the lobby is the ground floor, living-room-style Church Lounge, which is continuously ranked as one of the hippest places to hang out. Rooms are comfortable and outfitted with goodies such as Kiehl's bath products, Bose CD players and mini-TVs in the bathrooms. And since TriBeCa is the film district and the Tribeca Grand is a favorite of movie-industry types, there's even a screening room on the lower level.

number 73, map F **TRIBECA GRAND HOTEL**

ADDRESS 2 6th avenue, at church street **TELEPHONE** 212 519 6600 **WEBSITE** www.tribecagrand.com **CREDIT CARDS** visa, mastercard, amex **PRICE** from $250 **SUBWAY** c, e to canal street

One of your best bets for catching sight of a celebrity is to sink into an overstuffed sofa in the lobby of the Mercer and see who comes to check in. You may, after a certain point, start feeling like a stalker; that means it's time to check out the ever-delicious Mercer Kitchen, owned by famed chef Jean-Georges Vongerichten, or the Submercer bar downstairs. There are only 75 rooms, so if you're told that none is available it's probably not because your name isn't universally known… It could actually be that none is available. Rock stars and Hollywood bombshells love this hotel and, chances are, you will too.

ADDRESS 147 mercer street, at prince street **TELEPHONE** 212 966 6060 **WEBSITE** www.mercerhotel.com
CREDIT CARDS visa, mastercard, amex **PRICE** from $350 **SUBWAY** n, r to prince street

THE MERCER HOTEL number 74, map E

number 75, map C # MORGANS HOTEL

ADDRESS 237 madison avenue, between 37th and 38th streets **TELEPHONE** 212 686 0300 **WEBSITE** www.ianschragerhotels.com **PRICE** from $180 **SUBWAY** 4, 5, 6, 7, s to 42nd street/grand central

The Morgans Hotel is a study in quiet sophistication. The black-and-white lobby is understated and elegant, and the hotel manages to blend into the neighborhood without announcing itself with big signs and awnings. These are just some of the things that make Morgans an extremely popular hotel with the glitterati. Ever since it opened in 1984, the hotel and its accompanying Asia de Cuba restaurant and Morgans bar have been popular uptown alternatives to the glitz of SoHo. The hotel's proximity to the Empire State Building, Grand Central Station and Times Square also make it attractive to visitors.

ADDRESS 56 irving place, between 17th and 18th streets **TELEPHONE** 212 533 4600
WEBSITE www.innatirving.com **PRICE** from $295 **SUBWAY** l to 3rd avenue

INN AT IRVING PLACE number 76, map D

For Victorian charm in the heart of Manhattan, try the Inn at Irving Place. The hotel offers 12 rooms and suites furnished with beautiful period antiques and outfitted with modern amenities such as remote climate control and Internet access. Celebrities love the sophistication, luxury and total privacy offered by this hotel, set in an unmarked, 19th-century townhouse. The location is ideal, close to Union Square, Gramercy Park and all the pleasures of Greenwich Village, but this kind of refined gentility isn't cheap. If you can't afford to spend the night, consider spending the afternoon in Lady Mendl's tea parlor.

See the stars in all their naked glory at the new, ultra-modern Rose Center – the glass and steel extension to the American Museum of Natural History dedicated to stellar exploration. You don't have to be a space junkie to enjoy the exhibits, shows and jazz concerts held here; the ultra-contemporary interior design alone is worth the visit. Check out the hands-on, interactive exhibits, see a space show and witness the evolution of the universe in the Cosmic Pathway. The neighboring museum (your ticket includes admission to both) is also a charming and underrated cultural destination.

ROSE CENTER FOR EARTH AND SPACE

number 77, map A

ADDRESS west 81st street, between central park west and columbus avenue **TELEPHONE** 212 769 5200
WEBSITE www.amnh.org/rose **OPENING HOURS** sat-thu 10am-5.45pm, fri 10am-8.45pm **PRICE** $12
SUBWAY b, c to 81st street

shopping　　food & drink　　nightlife　　lodging　　culture　　various

ETHNI-CITY

THE GREAT MELTING POT

New York is a **city built on dreams**. The city owes its existence to immigrants, especially those who dared to dream. During the 1840s, the city's population increased by more than 60 percent and in the following ten years increased again by an additional 58 percent. People have always come here looking for a better life, and they still come in **search of opportunities** that might not exist in the country from which they came.

For immigrants arriving by ship in the 19th and early 20th centuries, the Statue of Liberty was the first signal that they had arrived in the "**promised land**." Soon after, they disembarked and were subjected to a **rigorous** and sometimes **traumatic screening process**. Passengers who had the money to travel in upper class were processed on the ship, but the rest were taken to the processing depot at **Ellis Island** to undergo painstaking medical tests and have their paperwork thoroughly checked.

Once the processing was complete, new arrivals took the **ferry to Lower Manhattan**, where they were responsible for finding a home, getting a job, seeking out new opportunities and very often quickly learning a new language. The part of the city south of 14th Street became **home to millions of immigrants** in the late 1800s and early 1900s. Most families lived in tenement houses – cramped, airless, over-crowded and often squalid buildings with one bathroom for every 20 people. These were the only affordable accommodations the city could offer at the time.

By the 1940s, most tenement apartments had bathrooms fitted into the kitchens and gas stoves to replace the previous coal-fired ones. These tenements still exist today, particularly on the **Lower East Side**. In fact, they've even become desirable with **young hipsters** and aren't exactly cheap to rent. These types of apartments are known as "**railroad flats**" because of the way the rooms are connected in a straight line, as if in a railroad car.

The Lower East Side is still home to immigrants, mostly from Puerto Rico and the **Dominican Republic**, but has mostly been taken over by **young, trendy bohemians**. There are other neighborhoods, however, that are so ethnic you'll feel **transported** by the preponderance of shops, restaurants and signage from one country or region. More and more these neighborhoods can be found outside of Manhattan, in places like the **Bronx, Brooklyn** and Queens.

Chinatown is one Manhattan neighborhood that persists in its **ethnicity**, although it should more accurately be called Asiatown because of the many Korean, Malaysian, Vietnamese and Indonesian establishments there.

Another enclave of ethnicity is West 46th Street, between 6th and 7th Avenues, long known as **"Little Brazil."** The **smell of Indian "masala"** commands the air in Jackson Heights, Queens, while just blocks away are the sights, sounds and smells of Latin America. Try Arthur Avenue in the Bronx for a small Little Italy or Atlantic Avenue in Brooklyn for Arabic culture. Brooklyn is also home to most of the city's **Caribbean** community.

One reason why New York is so appealing is that no matter where you come from, you're sure to find something here to **remind you of home**. Early immigrants came from Ireland, Germany, Italy, **Eastern Europe** and China, and while these cultures still take precedence over others, there's not a culture in the world that isn't somehow represented in New York. From **Azerbaijan** to Zanzibar, you can find it all here.

Some say the **diversity** of the city is best experienced through the **taste buds**. Eating your way around the world is easy in this city, as there's never a lack of exotic foods, and there's always a New Yorker willing to try something new. Try **exploring cuisines** you've never tasted before – everything is available in New York!

ETHNI-CITY

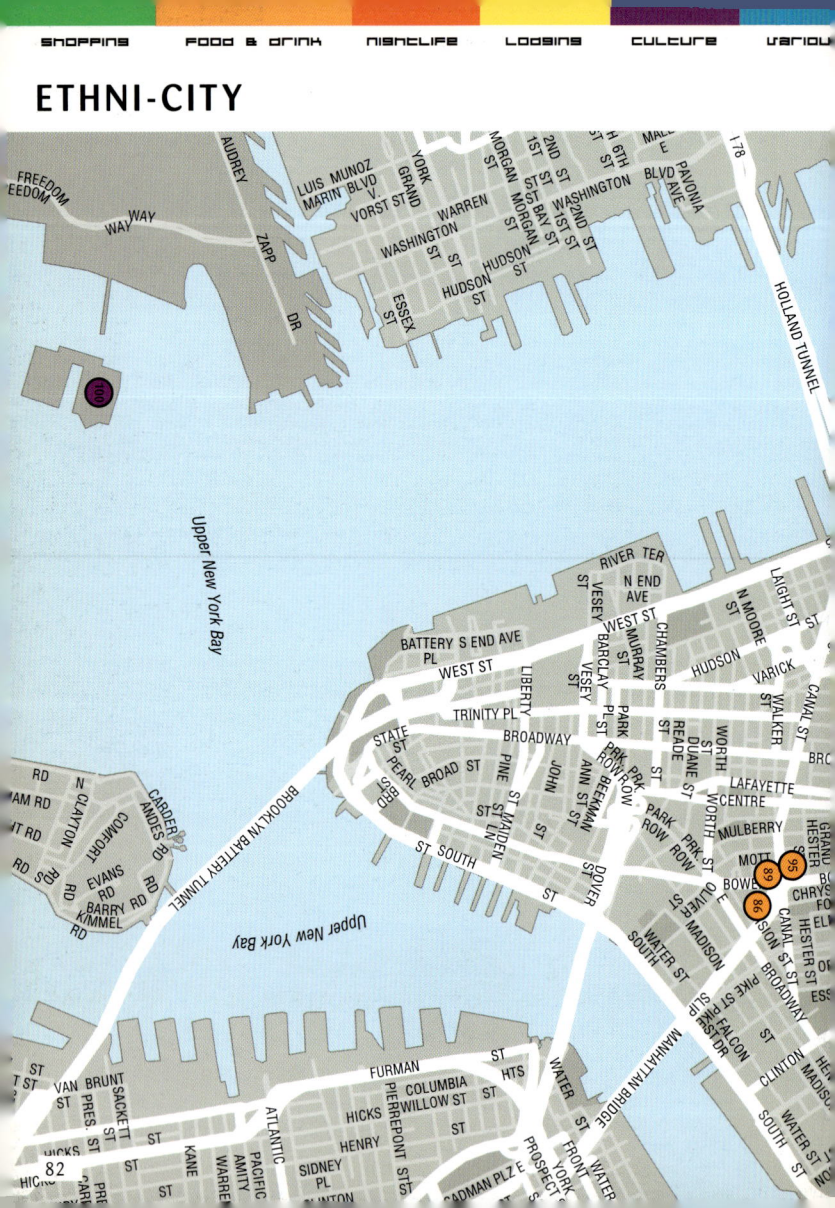

shopping · food & drink · nightlife · lodging · culture · various

SEE PAGE 206-213 FOR A MAP WITH ALL THE ADDRESSES FROM THIS GUIDE
(turn map 90°)

83

ADDRESS 179 east houston street, near orchard street **TELEPHONE** 212 475 4880 **WEBSITE** www.russanddaughters.com **OPENING HOURS** mon-sat 9am-7pm, sun 8am-5.30pm **SUBWAY** f to 2nd avenue

RUSS & DAUGHTERS number 84, map F

You'll find history and dedication to quality at this Lower East Side specialty food store. Established in 1914 by Joel Russ, an Eastern European immigrant who sold herrings from a pushcart when he first arrived in New York, the store is still family-run. Specialties include delicacies such as caviar, smoked fish and herring, as well as imported cheeses and other delectable goodies. Although this neighborhood used to be predominantly Jewish, it has changed dramatically, and this store is one of the last vestiges of how it used to be.

Chef Floyd Cardoz masterfully blends his French culinary training with his Indian heritage and North American surroundings to create a singularly refreshing menu. Tabla serves up Indian interpretations of Western treats like lobster, crab cakes, quail and "foie gras." A meal here is an adventure you won't soon forget. It begins as you walk in the lavish entrance and continues through each sumptuously prepared course. Upstairs is chic fine dining, but for something lighter and more casual, the downstairs Bread Bar is very popular, very hip and has a separate, but similarly inventive menu. Reservations are recommended for the restaurant, but are not accepted at the Bread Bar.

number 85, map C # TABLA

ADDRESS 11 madison avenue, at 25th street **TELEPHONE** 212 889 0667 **OPENING HOURS** restaurant: (lunch) mon-fri noon-2pm, (dinner) mon-sat 5.30-10.30pm, sun 5.30-9.30pm bread bar: mon-thu noon-11pm, fri noon-11.30pm, sat 5.30-11.30pm, sun 5.30-10pm **CREDIT CARDS** visa, mastercard, amex, diners club, discover **PRICE** restaurant: (lunch) $20 (dinner, prix fixe only) $45 bread bar: $20 **SUBWAY** 6, n, r to 23rd street

From the outside, it's hard to believe that this nondescript, cafeteria-style eatery is one of the best restaurants in Chinatown. New York Noodle Town offers great meals at great prices, and the huge bowls of noodle soup and heaping plates of barbecued pork are even available in the middle of the night. One look at the tables filled with Chinese families and hungry Wall Street workers is enough proof that the food is authentic and delicious. Menus are in English, but sadly the intriguing signs on the wall are not. Be sure to ask for help if you need it.

ADDRESS 28 bowery, at bayard street **TELEPHONE** 212 349 0923 **OPENING HOURS** daily 9-4am **PRICE** $10 **CREDIT CARDS** none **SUBWAY** j, m, n, r, z to canal street

NEW YORK NOODLETOWN number 86, map F

number 87, map C # GOLDEN KRUST BAKERY

ADDRESS several locations, including (1) grand central station, lower level (2) 18 east 33rd street, between madison and 5th avenues **TELEPHONE** (1) 646 487 2003 (2) 212 213 3824 **WEBSITE** www.goldenkrustbakery.com **OPENING HOURS** (1) mon-sat 10am-9pm, sun 10am-6pm (2) mon-fri 8am-8pm, sat 10am-6pm **CREDIT CARDS** none **PRICE** $2 **SUBWAY** (1) 4, 5, 6, 7, s to grand central (2) 6 to 33rd street

Jewish immigrants gave the city its passion for bagels, and Italians brought pizza, both of which are now beloved New York traditions. Immigrants from Jamaica have introduced the city to one of its newest obsessions: the Jamaican patty. It's a crispy, light pastry with a zesty beef, vegetable or chicken filling, and it's the specialty of the house at Golden Krust. This is a franchise operation with dozens of locations across the city offering an authentic Jamaican taste that won't disappoint. If you're really hungry, you'll probably need a couple to fill you up, so why not try one of each variety?

ADDRESS 30 east 13th street, between 5th avenue and university place **TELEPHONE** 646 336 1685
OPENING HOURS mon-sat 11am-10pm **CREDIT CARDS** none **PRICE** $10 **SUBWAY** 4, 5, 6, l, n, q, r, w to union square/14th street

DOSIRAK number 88, map C

Korean food has yet to become as ubiquitous as Chinese food in New York, but it's quietly and steadily gaining popularity amongst the gastronomically-curious. Many New Yorkers are already familiar with "bi bim bop," a rice, meat and vegetable dish served in a warm stone bowl and topped with a fried egg. Other dishes worth trying at Dosirak include noodles, hearty soups and a very spicy beef stew. Dosirak, which translates as "lunch box," is a simple, friendly, neighborhood restaurant that delivers good Korean food at reasonable prices. No alcohol is served, but feel free to bring your own.

shopping   food & drink   nightlife   lodging   culture   various

There are different levels to Sweet 'N' Tart, just as there are different menus. Upstairs in the red dining room, you can order traditional dim sum dumplings, meals and teas with curative and medicinal powers or more familiar-sounding Chinese dishes like noodles or hot-and-sour soup. Downstairs in the simple, brightly lit café, the same food is available in a more casual environment. The lower level interior might not look like much, but it's popular with a young, trendy Chinese crowd in search of delicious, uncomplicated food.

SWEET 'N' TART

number 89, map F

ADDRESS 76 mott street, at canal street **TELEPHONE** 212 334 8088 **OPENING HOURS** daily 9am-midnight **PRICE** $6 **CREDIT CARDS** none **SUBWAY** 6, j, m, z, n, q, r to canal street

89

There are many pizza joints in New York where you can grab a quick, greasy, cheesy slice. La Pizza Fresca is not one of them. This is an elegant, sit-down restaurant where pizza is taken very seriously and is made according to the standards of the "Associazione Verace Pizza Napoletana," the arbiter of authentic Naples-style pizza. The association's rules dictate that the pizzas use only "mozzarella di bufala" and ripe San Marzano tomatoes and are cooked in a wood-fired, 850-degree oven. This might sound strict, but the results are worth every mouthful. Your taste buds will thank you.

ADDRESS 31 east 20th street, between broadway and park avenue south **TELEPHONE** 212 598 0141
OPENING HOURS mon-fri noon-3.30pm, 5.30-11pm, sat 5.30-11pm, sun 5-11pm **PRICE** $13 **CREDIT CARDS** visa, mastercard, amex, discover **SUBWAY** 6, n, r, w to 23rd street

LA PIZZA FRESCA number 90, map C

shopping   food & drink   nightlife   lodging   culture   various

number 91, map E **NL**

ADDRESS 169 sullivan street, between bleecker and houston streets **TELEPHONE** 212 387 8801 **OPENING HOURS** daily 11am-11pm **PRICE** $15 **CREDIT CARDS** visa, mastercard, amex **SUBWAY** 1, 9 to houston street

Located in the city that was once called New Amsterdam, NL offers locals and travelers the tastes that New York's founding father (and famous Dutchman) Peter Stuyvesant knew and loved. Manhattan's only Dutch restaurant is appropriately decorated in shades of orange and features a tiled mosaic of Queen Beatrix on the wall. Enjoy traditional favorites like herring and smoked meats, or try an Indonesian-spiked dish, using spices from the country's former colony. The "rijsttafel" sampler plate – with its generous helpings of chicken satay, beef and beans – is a good place to start.

ADDRESS 28 greenwich avenue, between 10th and charles streets **TELEPHONE** 212 367 7411 **OPENING HOURS** daily 12.30-3.30pm, 5.30-10pm **PRICE** $10 **CREDIT CARDS** none **SUBWAY** a, c, e, f, v to west 4th street

THALI number 92, map E

Simplicity is the key to success at Thali. This West Village sliver of space only seats 20 people at a time and is decorated brightly, but sparsely. After selecting from several delicious a la carte appetizers, it's time to move on to the "thali," a stainless steel tray filled with a daily assortment of South Indian vegetarian dishes. Your tray will include two entrees (expect such things as cauliflower, eggplant, chickpeas and potatoes), rice, "dal," bread and one dessert. Lunch and dinner provide the same meal in different proportions, and alcohol is not served although you are welcome to bring your own.

shopping   food & drink   nightlife   lodging   culture   various

Since the 1960s, Americans haven't been allowed to travel to Cuba because of a political embargo. Instead, they have to satisfy themselves with tasting the food of the lush Caribbean island at one of the many restaurants in New York. Havana Central, with its fun, cafeteria-like ambiance, is one such place. Many say this is the best Cuban food in the city, easily rivaling that found in the much larger Cuban community of Miami. Try a "mojito," the classic Cuban cocktail, or a pitcher of sangria, and you're off to a good start. The tasty food is not only reasonably priced, it's hungry-man sized, too. Bring an appetite, and enjoy.

number 93, map C   # HAVANA CENTRAL

ADDRESS 22 east 17th street, between 5th avenue and broadway **TELEPHONE** 212 414 4999 **OPENING HOURS** mon-thu 11am-11pm, fri-sat 11am-midnight, sun noon-10pm **CREDIT CARDS** visa, mastercard, amex, diners club, discover **PRICE** $10 **SUBWAY** f, v to 14th street, l to 6th avenue

shopping　　food & drink　　nightlife　　lodging　　culture　　various

When Indian street food becomes popular on the New York club scene, you know you're living in a global village. Kati Rolls are cheap, inexpensive treats of spicy meat, potatoes or chicken wrapped in "parathas" (flat Indian bread). The rolls make a good snack or light meal during the week and are especially popular with late-night, after-partying crowds. (There are actually lines out the door and down the stairs between midnight and 4am). Don't plan to get too comfortable; there's just a counter and three tiny tables in the whole place. But that's OK, because Kati rolls are extremely portable.

ADDRESS 99 macdougal street, between bleecker and west 3rd streets **TELEPHONE** 212 420 6517 **OPENING HOURS** sun-thu 12.30pm-midnight, fri-sat 12.30pm-4am **CREDIT CARDS** visa, mastercard **PRICE** $5 **SUBWAY** a, c, e, f, v, s to west 4th street

KATI ROLL COMPANY number 94, map E

number 95, map F IL CORTILE

ADDRESS 125 mulberry street, between canal and hester streets **TELEPHONE** 212 226 6060 **WEBSITE** www.ilcortile.com **OPENING HOURS** mon-thu noon-midnight, fri-sat noon-1am, sun 1pm-midnight **CREDIT CARDS** visa, mastercard, amex **PRICE** $20 **SUBWAY** 6, j, m, n, q, r, w, z to canal street

Once upon a time, Little Italy was a lively ethnic neighborhood. Now, most of the Italians that grew up here generations ago have moved on to greener pastures, and the vestiges of the old neighborhood have become hackneyed and touristy. There are, however, a few bright lights amid the otherwise bland and unconvincing Italian restaurants on Mulberry Street. Il Cortile is one of them. The décor is just what you'd expect of Little Italy, with its faux frescoes and Roman statuary, but the food is top-quality and makes an outing to this once-vibrant neighborhood worth the trip.

ADDRESS 547 lenox avenue, between 137th and 138th streets **TELEPHONE** 212 690 3100 **OPENING HOURS** sun-thu 10.30am-9.30pm, fri-sat 10.30am-10pm **CREDIT CARDS** visa, mastercard, amex **PRICE** $11 **SUBWAY** 2, 3 to 135th street

MISS MAUDE'S SPOONBREAD TOO
number 96, map A

Miss Maude's Spoonbread Too features some of the best food in town, served with loads of Southern hospitality. If you think all New Yorkers are gruff, curt and unfriendly, you must not have been to Harlem yet! Walking in to Spoonbread is like going to a good friend's house for dinner. You'll be warmly welcomed and heartily fed. Soul food, the cuisine of the African-American south, is aptly named – who wouldn't feel warm, cozy and soul-satisfied after plate loads of short ribs, collard greens, fried chicken and mashed potatoes? Come in for Saturday or Sunday brunch and get your weekend off to a yummy, laid-back start.

Nouvelle Indian cuisine is in fine form at Surya, a cozy and elegant West Village restaurant. A sleek drinking lounge and polished wood bar greet you at the door, behind which is a long, modern dining room, pleasingly outfitted with ultra-suede banquettes, wood floors and dim lights. The menu is a tour of Southern Indian cuisine, the food that owner Raja Sethu grew up with. No beef is served, but there is a healthy selection of rice, vegetable, fish and lamb dishes to please every palate. Dishes are inventive and flavorful without overloading on fire-hot Indian spices. Wines are a bit pricey, but try one of the many beers, which beautifully complement the tasty food.

number 97, map E **SURYA**

ADDRESS 302 bleecker street, at 7th avenue south **TELEPHONE** 212 807 7770
OPENING HOURS mon-thu 6.30-11pm, fri-sat 6.30-11.30pm **CREDIT CARDS** visa, mastercard, amex
PRICE $18 **SUBWAY** 1, 9 to christopher street

shopping   food & drink   nightlife   lodging   culture   various

In 1900, 25 percent of the city's population was of German descent. These days, however, there are relatively few authentic German restaurants in the city. If names like "Weihenstephaner," "Hacker Pschorr" or "Würzburger Hofbräu" mean something to you, then you're bound to enjoy this indoor Bavarian beer hall on Manhattan's Lower East Side. Zum Schneider might not break any new culinary ground, but it's up there with the '"wurst" of them, successfully serving the typical sausage, potato and beer combination. Expect to find hip, lively music and an equally hip, lively young crowd.

ADDRESS 107 avenue c, at 7th street **TELEPHONE** 212 598 1098 **OPENING HOURS** mon-thu 5pm-2am, fri 4pm-4am, sun 1pm-2am **CREDIT CARDS** none **PRICE** $6 **SUBWAY** f, v to lower east side/2nd avenue, l to 1st avenue

ZUM SCHNEIDER number 98, map F

number 99, map D # **UNITED NATIONS**

ADDRESS 1st avenue, between 42nd and 46th streets **TELEPHONE** 212 963 8687 **OPENING HOURS** mon-fri 9.30am-4.45pm, sat-sun 10am-4.30pm (mon-fri only in jan and feb) **PRICE** $11 **SUBWAY** 4, 5, 6, 7, s to 42nd street/grand central

As you enter the gates of the United Nations Headquarters, you leave New York and the United States behind and enter international territory. The 18-acre site officially belongs not to one country, but to all countries that have joined the organization. The UN even has its own security and fire forces and issues its own postage stamps! A guided tour of the UN includes visits to the chambers of the Security Council and the main General Assembly Hall. Along the way, you will see countless pieces of art, including paintings, sculptures, tapestries and mosaics presented to the organization by member states.

ELLIS ISLAND IMMIGRATION MUSEUM number 100, map E

ADDRESS ellis island, new york harbor **TELEPHONE** 212 363 3206 **OPENING HOURS** daily 9.30am-5pm
PRICE $10 **SUBWAY** n, r to whitehall, 4, 5 to bowling green, then ferry to ellis island

More than 70 percent of the immigrants who came to the U.S. in the 19th and 20th centuries landed in New York, and most of them were processed at Ellis Island. Between 1892 and 1954, the depot processed approximately twelve million immigrants and has now become symbolic of the immigrant experience. The museum tells the story of this courageous journey through displays of artifacts like baggage, clothing, passports, tickets and ship's manifests and the halls where immigrants were subjected to legal and medical inspections. The ferry ride out there is a trip in itself, offering excellent views of New York Harbor, the Statue of Liberty and the Manhattan skyline.

shopping   food & drink   nightlife   lodging   culture   various

There are many places in the city to have a Middle Eastern meal, but few beat the charming outdoor "garden" at Sahara East for ambiance. In New York (especially in the East Village), "garden" is loosely defined as any space without four walls and a roof. Sahara's garden is tented and atmospheric, and how can you argue with the mellow, mood-enhancing effects of a flavored "shisha?" Get a hookah for the table, and choose from tobacco flavored with melon, mango, apple, honey or vanilla, among others. On weekends, you may be treated to a belly-dancing beauty or Moroccan disco music. Either way, it's bound to be an experience.

ADDRESS 184 1st avenue, between 11th and 12th streets **TELEPHONE** 212 353 9000 **OPENING HOURS** daily 11-1am **CREDIT CARDS** none **PRICE** $12 **SUBWAY** l to 1st avenue

number 101, map D   # SAHARA EAST

ADDRESS 155 west 13th street **TELEPHONE** 212 691 7314 **OPENING HOURS** tour times vary
PRICE approximately $115

SAVORY SOJOURNS number 102, map C

Explore the best tastes of the city with Addie Tomei of Savory Sojourns by your side. She'll arrange to take you on a tour of the city the way only a local can. You'll hit the streets of the Lower East Side, Greenwich Village and the Meat Packing District or cross one of the rivers to the Outer Boroughs, where Addie will show you the Italian district of the Bronx or Brooklyn's Atlantic Avenue. While you're on your tour, you can ask Addie about her daughter Marisa, the Academy Award winning actress!

notes

shopping　　food & drink　　nightlife　　lodging　　culture　　various

SINGLE IN THE CITY

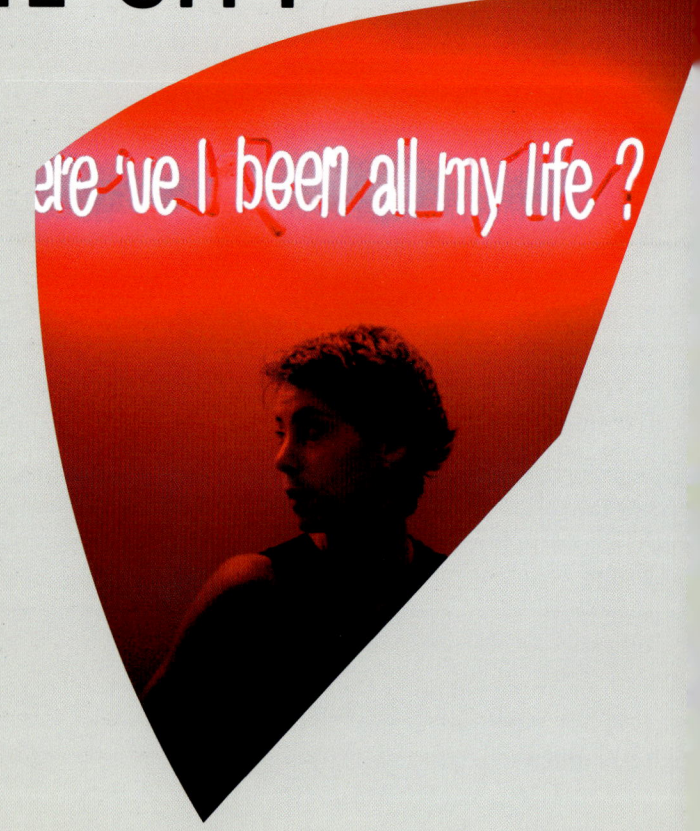

shopping   food & drink   nightlife   lodging   culture   various

MEET YOUR MATCH

Never before has being **single in New York** been as hyped as it is right now, thanks in large part to the universal popularity of HBO's "Sex and the City." The show attracted millions of viewers around the world by following the highly romanticized and **hormone-driven lives** of four sassy, sexy single women in Manhattan. The ladies lived in apartments most single working women would only dream of owning, took **frequent shoe shopping** trips that would cost the equivalent of a month's salary and never seemed to worry about "opposite-side-of-the-street parking." Must be nice!

One true reflection of the show is that **one out of every three adults** in New York City is single. You might think, with such a pool to pick from, that it would be easy to meet your soul mate, but most single New Yorkers would attest to the fact that **meeting Mr. or Mrs. Right** is an uphill battle. City life is competitive, and people can be aggressive or aloof. Plus, many young singles are so focused on their **careers** that they have little time to invest in their personal lives. When they do go out to find each other, they often don't know where to look. Bars and nightclubs are magnets for people looking for **quick flings,** but not exactly the perfect breeding ground for marital bliss.

Thus, New Yorkers figure out other **ways to meet each other**. They not only participate in activities they enjoy, hoping to meet other singles with similar interests, they **join clubs** such as the "single mountain bikers club" or the "single classical music club," where they feel they are bound to make a **mental match**.

Dating services are another popular way for singles to find each other. In the Internet age, singles simply have to log on to their computers to browse thousands of potential dates, read their profiles and see their photos. Another new trend is **speed dating**, where single men and women sign up to go on dozens of organized "dates" in one night. These events, which take place in some of the trendiest restaurants and bars around the city, register equal numbers of single men and women ahead of time. Everyone spends **three minutes** talking to each other and gives each date a score – if you pick someone and he or she picks you too, you've got a match, and the organizers will help you arrange to meet again.

Museums, cafés and **bookstores** have also been lauded as **good spots** for meeting like-minded people. This is a far less structured environment than a speed date, so it takes some courage and gumption to strike up a conversation. New Yorkers are not **shy people** though, so timidity rarely poses a problem. If you're happily sipping a cup of coffee or browsing the shelves of a bookstore when someone approaches you and **starts to chat**, don't be alarmed… Be flattered.

But don't jump to conclusions or start picking out names for your **unborn children**. The person may not be looking for anything more than a brief conversation. Open up, and you may find yourself engrossed in a **fascinating** (or at the very least entertaining) **conversation**. What happens next is up to you.

On the **bar scene**, singles (especially single men) can be much more **aggressive**. Urban sophisticates or not, many of them are **interested in one thing** only and often don't seem to understand the subtleties of the word "no." Learn to be **firm** if you're not interested or you may end up with more than you bargained for.

SINGLE IN THE CITY

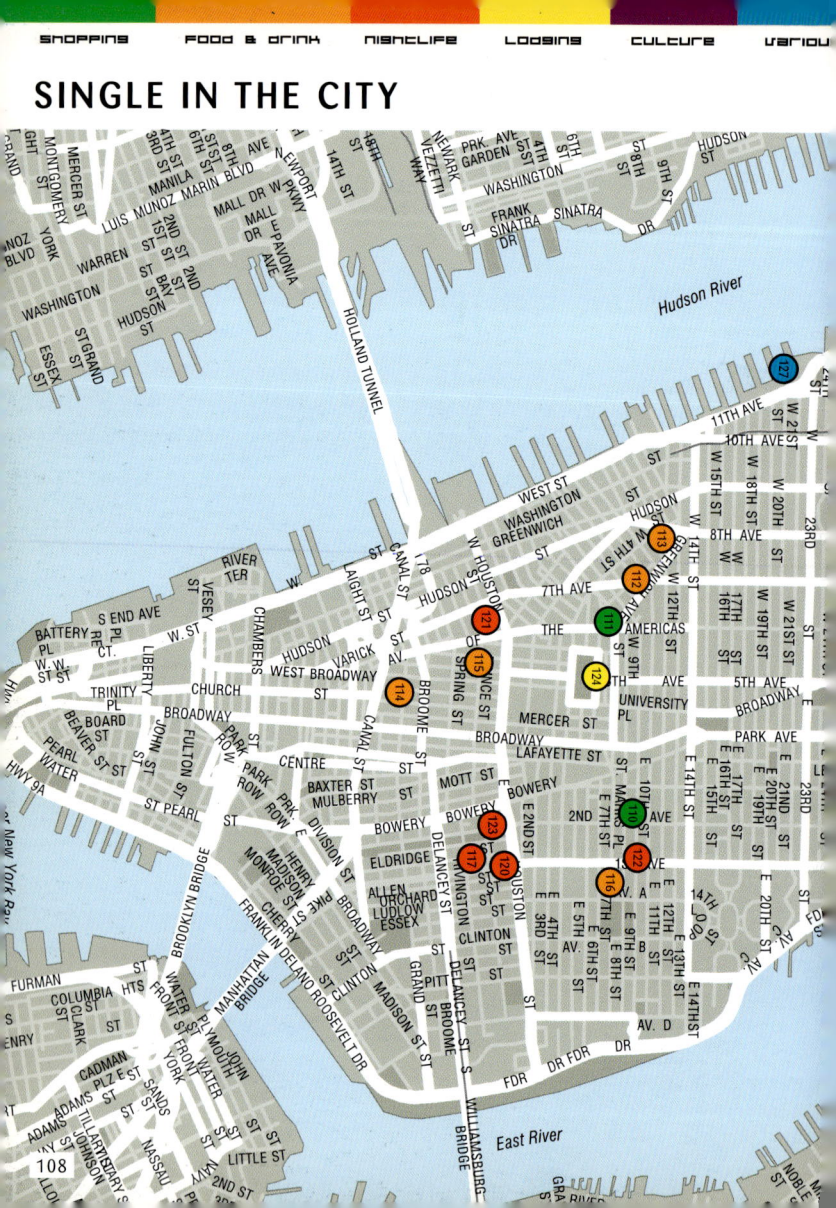

SEE PAGE 206-213 FOR A MAP WITH ALL THE ADDRESSES FROM THIS GUIDE
(turn map 90°)

109

ADDRESS 31 3rd avenue, at 9th street **TELEPHONE** 212 260 7853 **WEBSITE** www.stmarksbookshop.com
OPENING HOURS mon-sat 10am-midnight, sun 11am-midnight **SUBWAY** 6 to astor place, l to 3rd avenue, n, r to 8th street

ST. MARK'S BOOKSTORE

number 110, map F

This small, independent bookstore is brimming with alternative publications and books on cultural and critical theory, art, photography and music. If you're looking to rub shoulders with East Village radicals, New York intellectuals or students from nearby New York University or Cooper Union, you've come to the right place. This is the bookstore for intelligent people – no pulpy romance novels or brainless fiction here. Soak in the alternative, intellectual spirit of the East Village before it gets completely usurped by mindless consumerism courtesy of McDonald's and the Gap (both of which have recently moved in nearby).

shopping | food & drink | nightlife | lodging | culture | various

Lingerie has to be the most egalitarian of all articles of clothing. It makes women happy – they look and feel sexy. For men, what's not to like? And even if you're single, it doesn't mean you can't look and feel great all the time. In that spirit, Laina Jane offers a healthy selection of sexy, name-brand lingerie in a range of styles, colors and prices. This is a no-nonsense store with knowledgeable staff and great selection – even actress Liv Tyler shops here! Who knows, a visit to Laina Jane might mean you won't be single much longer.

number 111, map A **LAINA JANE**

ADDRESS (1) 416 amsterdam avenue, near 80th street (2) 35 christopher street, near waverly place **TELEPHONE** (1) 212 875 9168 (2) 212 727 7032 **CREDIT CARDS** visa, mastercard, amex **SUBWAY** (1) 1, 9 to 79th street, b, c to 81st street (2) 1, 9 to christopher street

shopping　　food & drink　　nightlife　　lodging　　culture　　various

At this West Village hideaway, customers can while away an entire day. There's plenty of art to explore, books to read (grab one off the shelf if you don't have one) and coffee, wine and beer to drink. The café/gallery is a popular spot with telecommuters who pound away on their laptops and study groups who chat about lofty subjects. As a single, you can enjoy sitting quietly or chatting with other customers, depending on how sociable you feel. Try the panini sandwiches, cakes or salads, which are all fresh and delicious.

ADDRESS 17 perry street, at 7th avenue south **TELEPHONE** 212 929 4339 **OPENING HOURS** daily 7.30am-midnight **CREDIT CARDS** none **PRICE** average sandwich $7 **SUBWAY** 1, 9 to christopher street/sheridan square

DOMA CAFÉ AND GALLERY　number 112, map E

… shopping … food & drink … nightlife … lodging … culture … various

number 113, map E MAGNOLIA BAKERY

ADDRESS 401 bleecker street, at 11th street **TELEPHONE** 212 462 2572 **OPENING HOURS** mon noon-11.30pm, tue-thu 9am-11.30pm, fri 9-12.30am, sat 10-12.30am, sun 10am-11.30pm **CREDIT CARDS** none **PRICE** cupcake $3 **SUBWAY** a, c, e to 14th street

Come for a cupcake, leave with no teeth. OK, that's a bit of an exaggeration, but the sickeningly sweet treats and West Village hipster patrons are what make Magnolia Bakery a real hot spot. The freshly baked desserts hearken back to the 1950s "Leave It to Beaver" era – loads of butter, highly refined white flour, sugar and icing – and have created what many describe as a "cultish" following in the neighborhood. Buy a coffee, cupcake, mini cheesecake or a slice of delectable German chocolate cake, and linger for a while. Remember, the best route to the heart is through the stomach!

ADDRESS 59 grand street, between west broadway and wooster street **TELEPHONE** 212 941 0772 **OPENING HOURS** sun-thu noon-2am, fri-sat noon-4am **PRICE** $13 **CREDIT CARDS** visa, mastercard, amex, diners club **SUBWAY** a, c, e to canal street

LUCKY STRIKE number 114, map E

Supermodels and the fabulously famous once tucked themselves away here to escape paparazzi and other celebrity seekers. These days, crowds still throng to Lucky Strike – whether they're famous or not. They come for the shabby chic, faux-French interior, affordable bistro food and retro cocktail menu. The cozy tables in the back are the best place to watch the beautiful crowds, especially on weekends when DJs spin funky tunes. Grab a few Lucky Martinis, and you might just get lucky yourself.

shopping　　food & drink　　nightlife　　lodging　　culture　　various

This classy, sunny corner café is a hip hangout for posh singles. The wood bar and cozy banquettes are the perfect place for mingling with corporate hot shots over after-work cocktails. The café is also popular for brunch, which draws huge crowds and long lines. The food is good, but not mind-blowing, and it's best to stick with simple selections like a roast turkey club sandwich or bacon-wrapped meatloaf. Sink into your seat, and savor the views of the SoHo streets outside and the eye candy inside.

number 115, map E **CUB ROOM CAFÉ**

ADDRESS 183 prince street, at sullivan street **TELEPHONE** 212 677 4100 **OPENING HOURS** sun-thu 10-2am, fri-sat 10-4am **PRICE** $13 **CREDIT CARDS** visa, mastercard, amex, diners club **SUBWAY** c, e to spring street

shopping food & drink nightlife lodging culture various

She might be stingy, but not when it comes to food. Portions at this East Village diner are certainly big enough to satisfy the midnight munchies most people come here for. In the wee hours of the morning, when neon lights make faces glow in strange ways, it's even harder to tell whether your waitress is a woman or a man in drag. But then, it doesn't really matter – the prices are cheap, the company is friendly and hip, and the coffee is hot and fresh.

ADDRESS 129 st mark's place, between 1st avenue and avenue a **TELEPHONE** 212 674 3445 **OPENING HOURS** mon-fri 11-4am, sat-sun 10-4am **PRICE** $10 **CREDIT CARDS** none **SUBWAY** 6 to astor place

STINGY LULU'S number 116, map F

shopping   food & drink   nightlife   lodging   culture   various

number 117, map E # PEOPLE

ADDRESS 163 allen street, between stanton and rivington streets **TELEPHONE** 212 254 2668 **WEBSITE** www.peoplelounge.com **OPENING HOURS** mon-fri 5.30pm-3am, sat-sun 7pm-3am **CREDIT CARDS** visa, mastercard, amex, discover **PRICE** average drink $8 **SUBWAY** f, v to lower east side/2nd avenue

New York's best up-and-coming neighborhood for nightlife is the Lower East Side and one of the neighborhood's newest attractions is People. This towering, unpretentious two-level bar is pleasingly decorated and features an 18-foot red mahogany bar downstairs and a matching sidebar on the mezzanine level, as well as a water cascade, rows of banquette seating and floor-to-ceiling windows. People offers light appetizers and plenty of opportunity for people-watching. The comprehensive drink menu is decently priced and served by friendly staff and hip, DJ-spun tunes play on weekends. Call ahead to find out drink specials and guest DJs.

ADDRESS hudson hotel, 356 west 58th street, between 8th and 9th avenues **TELEPHONE** 212 554 6317
WEBSITE www.ianschragerhotels.com **OPENING HOURS** daily noon-4am **CREDIT CARDS** visa, mastercard, amex, discover **SUBWAY** 1, 9, a, b, c, d to 59th street/columbus circle

LIBRARY BAR number 118, map C

Hotel bars have become hip hangouts, and one of the hippest is at midtown's Hudson Hotel – the most mod of any hotel in the neighborhood. Guests can mingle with trendy city-dwellers in two bars – the beautifully lit and ultra-hip Hudson Bar or the more laidback Library Bar. The Library's centerpiece is a purple pool table with a dramatically oversized dome lamp. Although there are a few art and design books left on tables for good measure, most of the volumes are out of reach. (You didn't really want to read, did you?) Fireplaces, wood paneling and leather club chairs complete the effect.

shopping   food & drink   nightlife   lodging   culture   various

The cavernous Cellar Bar, which features a vaulted ceiling, medieval chandeliers, yellow ottomans and soft lighting is a unique spot to meet singles in New York. The ambiance is further enhanced by the Mediterranean-inspired bar and its 21-page drink menu with alcoholic concoctions from every corner of the globe. Particularly popular are the black cherry-topped "Cellar Sling" and the "Razmopolitan," and with such a huge selection you won't have to worry about running out of options. Should hunger strike, the high caliber of drinks is matched by deliciously creative (and decadent) bar food and even tasty desserts. Dress to impress, because this bar fills with stylish singles on weekends.

number 119, map C # CELLAR BAR

ADDRESS bryant park hotel, 40 west 40th street, between 5th and 6th avenues **TELEPHONE** 212 642 2260
OPENING HOURS daily 11-3am **CREDIT CARDS** visa, mastercard, amex **PRICE** average drink $11
SUBWAY 7 to 5th avenue, b, d, f, q to 42nd st

Bob's definitely not your uncle, but rather a tiny, hole-in-the-wall club on a rather dreary Lower East Side street. It's a very popular hangout for guys and girls who like to grind to hip-hop and reggae tunes. The lack of space puts everyone in close proximity to each other, and, when combined with the high sex drive of most of the customers, Bob's definitely not for the faint of heart or the claustrophobic. The work of local artists decorates the walls of this cramped space, but the main emphasis is on drinking, dancing and meeting members of the opposite sex.

BOB number 120, map F

ADDRESS 235 eldridge street, between houston and stanton streets **TELEPHONE** 212 777 0588
OPENING HOURS daily 7pm-4am **PRICE** average drink $6 **SUBWAY** f, v to lower east side/2nd avenue

shopping   food & drink   nightlife   lodging   culture   various

number 121, map E # CULTURE CLUB

ADDRESS 179 varick street, between king and charlton streets **TELEPHONE** 212 243 1999 **OPENING HOURS** thu-sat 9pm-5am **CREDIT CARDS** visa, mastercard, amex **PRICE** average drink $6 **SUBWAY** 1, 9 to houston street

Great for a girl's night out or when you're looking to dance the night away, Culture Club has stopped time in the 1980s. Even though it's taken the theme to an extreme, with absolutely no sense of subtlety, when you walk in, you know exactly what to expect: Pac Man, the Breakfast Club and Boy George adorn the walls, as do other obvious symbols of the Reagan era. The music, though predictable, is fun, and the dance floor is perennially packed with ladies dancing to the songs they grew up with. If you enjoyed the 80's and don't mind a time warp back, you'll likely have a great time.

ADDRESS 332 east 11th street, between 1st and 2nd avenues **TELEPHONE** 212 677 1027 **WEBSITE** www.cinemaclassics.com **OPENING HOURS** bar mon-thu 6pm-2am, fri-sat noon-4am **PRICE** average drink $5 **SUBWAY** l to 1st avenue

RIFIFI number 122, map F

If your idea of a fun night out includes more than just boozing in a bar, check out Rififi. Named after a 1955 film noir classic about a botched jewel heist, this East Village venue is part of a larger complex called Cinema Classics that includes a video store and movie theater. Rififi hosts comedy and burlesque shows, movies and DJ nights including Trash! (the best in Britpop and new wave) and Blister (classic rock anthems and alternative pop). The crowd at Rififi is artistic, individualistic and a little bit out there. But hey, that's what makes it a very New York experience!.

shopping　　food & drink　　nightlife　　lodging　　culture　　various

At 17 Home, you'll find all the style of a hip, Lower East Side bar with less attitude than many of the places surrounding it. Ladies will feel particularly welcome and benefit from drink specials and lots of male attention. The DJ spins hip-hop and soul, and the crowd is mellow and laid back. If the front lounge gets too crowded, no problem: Head towards the tented back room, which opens to the heavens in summer. Come on in, grab a table, and make yourself at home.

number 123, map F

17 HOME

ADDRESS 17 stanton street, between chrystie street and bowery **TELEPHONE** 212 598 2145 **OPENING HOURS** tue-sat 5pm-4am **CREDIT CARDS** visa, mastercard, amex, discover **PRICE** average drink $8
SUBWAY f, v to lower east side/2nd avenue

The charming and historic Washington Square Hotel is located right in the heart of Greenwich Village. The recently renovated hotel features 165 guest rooms and daily complimentary breakfast. In the lobby is the Art Deco-style Café Vogue, which serves light food, afternoon tea and cocktails. Other facilities include a massage room and fitness center. But the real draw is the neighborhood – staying here puts you steps away from world-famous jazz clubs, eclectic restaurants, trendy shops and everything else this area has to offer. Washington Square Park, which acts as backyard to residents of the Village, is at your doorstep – a claim no other hotel can make.

ADDRESS 103 waverly place, at washington square **TELEPHONE** 212 777 9515 (reservations) 800 222 0418 **WEBSITE** www.wshotel.com **PRICE** from $160 **SUBWAY** 1, 9 to christopher street, a, c, e, f, v to west 4th street

WASHINGTON SQUARE HOTEL

number 124, map E

shopping   food & drink   nightlife   Lodging   culture   various

number 125, map C # GERSHWIN HOTEL

ADDRESS 7 east 27th street **TELEPHONE** 212 545 8000 **WEBSITE** www.gershwinhotel.com **PRICE** from $99
SUBWAY 6 to 28th street

When you walk in the lobby and see the designer furniture and autographed Andy Warhol painting on the wall, you might think you've entered a high-priced, artsy boutique hotel. That is the beauty of the Gershwin. This hotel is in fact a budget traveler's dream, with private, minimalist rooms or dormitory-style hostel accommodations at some of the lowest prices in town. Beyond the pop art and the unique façade, the hotel also features an art gallery and an in-house cabaret with a rotating schedule of live music, stand-up comedy and theatrical performances several nights a week.

ADDRESS 1071 5th avenue, at 89th street **TELEPHONE** 212 423 3500 **WEBSITE** www.guggenheim.org
OPENING HOURS sat-wed 10am-5.45pm, fri 10am-8pm **PRICE** $15 **SUBWAY** 4, 5, 6 to 86th street

GUGGENHEIM MUSEUM number 126, map A

Spend the day at the Guggenheim, one of New York's most famous museums, and you are bound to fall in love. You may not leave the museum with a marriage proposal in hand, but you will almost certainly leave with newfound respect and admiration, not only for the impressive collection of art housed inside, but for the building itself. Standing out amongst the staid but stately apartment towers of 5th Avenue, Frank Lloyd Wright's corkscrew-shaped design turned heads when it was built in the 1950s and continues to do so to this day.

shopping   food & drink   nightlife   lodging   culture   various

For the active single, Chelsea Piers is amazing. What better way to meet a like-minded individual than doing something you both love, whether that's golfing, skating, playing basketball or football, roller-skating, rock climbing or bowling? Chelsea Piers has all that and more… There's a restaurant, a bar, a marina, a board-and-skate shop, film and television studios and even a full-service spa. As the motto says: "You Gotta See This Place."

number 127, map C **CHELSEA PIERS**

ADDRESS piers 59-62, 23rd street at hudson river **TELEPHONE** 212 336 6666 **WEBSITE** www.chelseapiers.com **OPENING HOURS & PRICE** vary by activity **SUBWAY** c, e to 23rd street

shopping   food & drink   nightlife   lodging   culture   variou

If you've ever met someone and known within three minutes that you don't want to see him or her ever again, speed dating is perfect for you. It's like having 25 dates in one night! Have your witty conversation ready, because when your three minutes are up the whistle blows and you're off. Take your scorecard with you, and rate each person based on whether or not you'd see them again. If they say yes to you too you're a match! Even if you don't meet anyone, the worst that can happen is you spend a night in a cool bar or lounge meeting people you otherwise wouldn't talk to. Think of the stories!

ADDRESS locations of parties vary **TELEPHONE** 212 871 6707 **WEBSITE** hurrydate.com **CREDIT CARDS** visa, mastercard, amex **PRICE** $37

HURRY DATE   locations vary

notes

shopping | food & drink | nightlife | lodging | culture | various

GROOVIN' GOTHAM

WHERE MUSICAL HISTORY IS MADE

From Beethoven to battle of the bands, opera to **open mic**, klezmer to **karaoke**: When it comes to music, New York City truly has it all. Whether you enjoy listening to a symphony in the park or a garage band in a **basement**, your pleasures will all be indulged in the Big Apple.

It's said that even the nickname **"Big Apple"** finds its **roots** in a **musical tradition**. The phrase was widely used amongst jazz musicians in the 30s and 40s as a metaphor for achieving success. The thinking was that there are many apples on a tree – smaller gigs in smaller cities – but when you picked New York, you picked the Big Apple. Getting the chance to **play gigs** in New York, especially in the theaters of Harlem or on Broadway, was reaching **the heights of success**.

Musicians have come to this city from then on in search of **fame and fortune**; a walk past the Juilliard School or down practically any street in the East Village shows that not much has changed in this regard. Some come for formal training, some gain insight through trial and error, but either way the city is undeniably full of **creativity, talent and youthful enthusiasm**.

Broadway is still the place to witness the **birth of a star**. The very name **Broadway** has become synonymous with musical theater, and quality

shopping   Food & drink   nightlife   Lodging   culture   various

productions abound. Pop music stars and screen actors are often headlining acts, and big names sell out well in advance. (Even if musicals don't float your boat, there is a wonderful selection of **dramatic performance** on Broadway, off-Broadway and even off-off-Broadway.)

For **classical music**, Carnegie Hall and Lincoln Center offer opportunities to see some of the biggest names in the business in truly elegant surroundings. With twelve independent resident companies, Lincoln Center for the Performing Arts is the **largest cultural complex** in the world. This is the home of the world-renowned Metropolitan Opera, the Chamber Music Society, the New York City Ballet, the New York Philharmonic and the Juilliard School.

One Central Park – the huge, new building at Columbus Circle, with its apartments, hotel rooms, offices, stores and restaurants – is also the new home of **Jazz at Lincoln Center**. Led by Artistic Director **Wynton Marsalis**, Jazz at Lincoln Center is dedicated to the appreciation and understanding of jazz through performance, education and preservation.

Harlem remains the **spiritual home of jazz** in New York, as well as the physical home of many successful rap and hip-hop stars. Some of the best and

| shopping | food & drink | nightlife | lodging | culture | various |

most popular jazz clubs are now farther downtown, but nothing beats the experience of a night out in a **Harlem nightclub**. History combines beautifully with the spirit and rhythm of the music to make for an **unforgettable experience**. Many of the most famous clubs of the 30s and 40s – places like Small's Paradise – have now been closed down, but their **legends and legacies** live on in Harlem.

For **rock,** pop, alternative or **punk** music just hit the streets of the East Village and Lower East Side, and **follow your ears** – you'll be treated to an endless selection of **live music**. The most popular dance clubs are also located in this neighborhood, as well as along 14th Street.

Check out the **Village Voice** or **New York Press**, two free weekly newspapers, for listings of cultural events, concerts and DJ appearances. The Village Voice is available in bright-red street-side boxes and comes out on Wednesdays, while the NY Press is in green boxes and is issued on Tuesdays.

NOTE: Several of the club listings in this chapter require advance ticket purchase and may have cover charges. You are strongly recommended to call ahead for additional information.

GROOVIN' GOTHAM

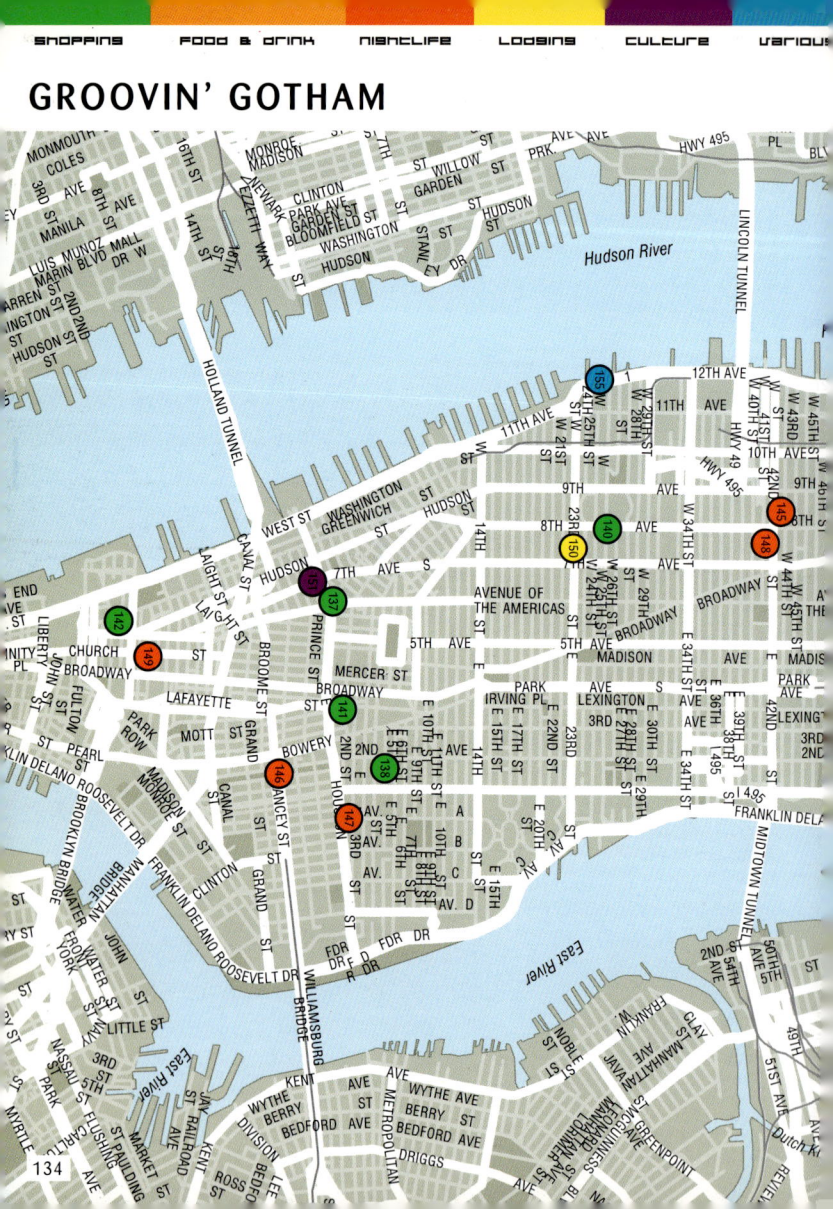

134

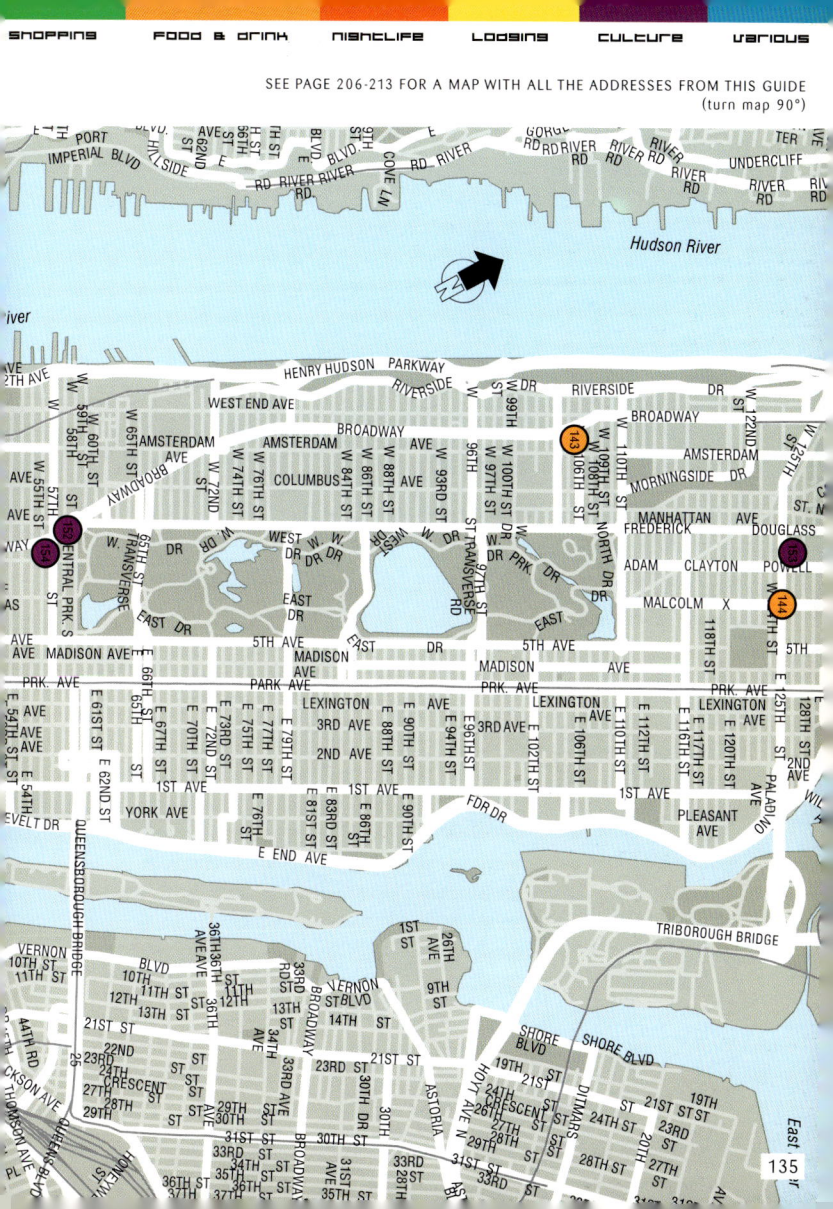

shopping | food & drink | nightlife | lodging | culture | various

SEE PAGE 206-213 FOR A MAP WITH ALL THE ADDRESSES FROM THIS GUIDE
(turn map 90°)

135

ADDRESS 1619 broadway, at 49th street **TELEPHONE** 212 265 2050 **WEBSITE** www.colonymusic.com
OPENING HOURS mon-sat 9.30-1am, sun 10am-midnight **SUBWAY** n, r to 49th street

COLONY MUSIC CENTER number 136, map C

For Broadway music soundtracks and scores, Colony is one-stop shopping. Its location is a dead giveaway – right at the top end of Times Square, the heart of the Theater District. Stop in if you're looking for sheet music or vintage vinyl recordings of your favorite musicals. The shop, which has been around since 1948, used to be located on West 52nd Street, also known as "Swing Street." Back then, the legendary Birdland Jazz Club was across the street, and people like Miles Davis, Charlie Parker and Ella Fitzgerald were regular customers, trusting Colony to provide them with the raw materials to build their burgeoning careers.

shopping   food & drink   nightlife   lodging   culture   various

You know what you're in for when you step into Vinylmania. Vinyl, vinyl and more... Well, you know (although there is a small room with CDs in the back). DJs come to this West Village outpost to flesh out their collections and search the racks for house, trance, acid jazz, garage and dance classics. You can accessorize your DJ self here too, with everything you need plus many things you don't. Fans of modern dance music are bound to find something that strikes a chord (if you'll excuse the silly pun).

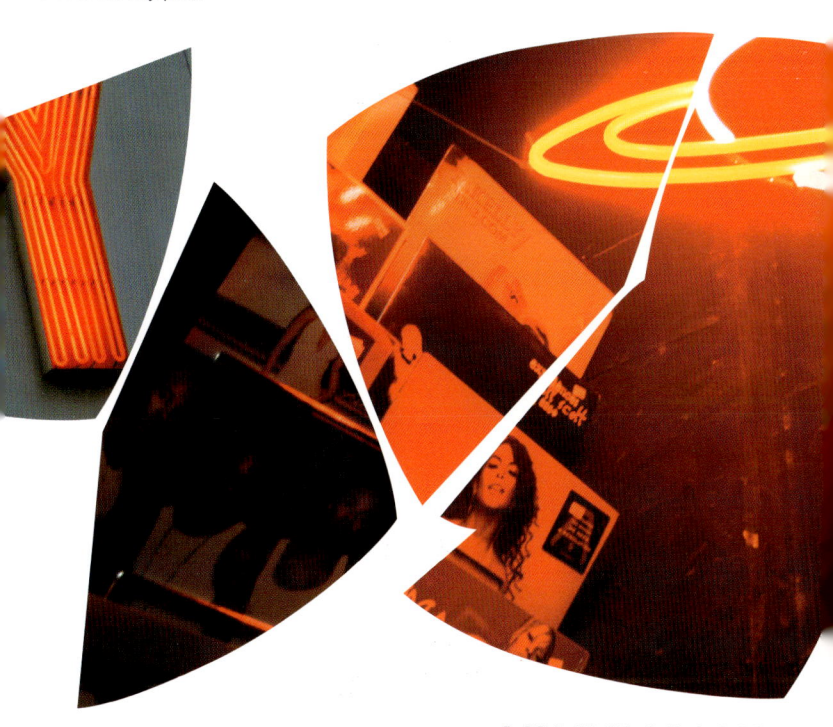

number 137, map E **VINYLMANIA**

ADDRESS 60 carmine street, near bedford street **TELEPHONE** 212 924 7223 **WEBSITE** www.vinylmania.com
OPENING HOURS mon-sat 11am-9pm, sun 11am-7pm

shopping   food & drink   nightlife   lodging   culture   various

If a street can have a persona, then St. Mark's Place would be a punk. Although it's much harder these days to find kids who are willing to spend hours spiking their hair into the perfect Mohawk, back in the heyday of the movement this street – especially the block between 1st and 2nd Avenues – was punk headquarters. Appropriately, Wowsville is located smack dab in this legendary location. This used record and CD store carries an excellent selection of punk, hardcore, new wave and garage music, as well as concert tickets, accessories and t-shirts (black, of course).

WOWSVILLE number 138, map F

ADDRESS 125 2nd avenue, between st. mark's place and 7th street **TELEPHONE** 212 654 0935 **WEBSITE** www.wowsville.net **SUBWAY** f, v to 2nd avenue

shopping   food & drink   nightlife   lodging   culture   various

number 139, map C ## SAM ASH MUSIC

ADDRESS 160 west 48th street, between 6th & 7th avenues **TELEPHONE** 212 719 2299
WEBSITE www.samashmusic.com **OPENING HOURS** mon-fri 10am-8pm, sat 10am-7pm, sun noon-6pm
SUBWAY n, r to 49th street

Located on a block known as "Guitar Row," Sam Ash is one of the largest music stores in the city and can provide you with practically every musical item you need. The only thing they can't sell is talent, but at least you can load up on inspiration. The contiguous stores sell literally everything you can imagine: professional sound equipment, sheet music, drums and percussion instruments, guitars, keyboards, recording gear, computers, software and lighting. There's even a dedicated DJ department. The selection of guitars is really impressive, including Les Pauls and Stratocasters. I've heard the Rolling Stones shop here when they're in town. Enough said.

ADDRESS 236 west 26th street, suite 804, between 7th and 8th avenues **TELEPHONE** 212 675 4480
WEBSITE www.jazzrecordcenter.com **OPENING HOURS** mon-sat 10am-6pm (closed sat in summer)
CREDIT CARDS visa, mastercard, discover **SUBWAY** 1, 9 to 28th street, c, e to 23rd street

JAZZ RECORD CENTER number 140, map C

Buy and sell jazz and blues LPs, CDs, books, videos and magazines at this West Side hideaway. The selection in this aboveground store is magnificent, with a wide array of rare and out-of-print records and some of the best jazz around. Available labels include Blue Note, Clef, New Jazz, Prestige and Transition. You can also pick up back issues of jazz magazines like Downbeat and Metronome and other jazz collectibles, such as t-shirts, posters and calendars, as well as tour books and concert programs.

shopping | food & drink | nightlife | lodging | culture | various

Other Music sets the pace for many music fans, delivering exactly what they're looking for in a simple (if small) store located steps from New York University, the East Village and the Lower East Side. Eclectic is definitely the way to describe the selection in this store, which mostly carries CDs, but also has some vinyl. You'll find everything from indie rock to free jazz, electronica and Japanese releases. Sign up for the email newsletter, which will apprise you of what's new on the shelves that week. Shipping is available to international locations, so you can continue to fill out your collection even after your vacation is over.

number 141, map E **OTHER MUSIC**

ADDRESS 15 east 4th street, between broadway and lafayette streets **TELEPHONE** 212 477 8150
WEBSITE www.othermusic.com **OPENING HOURS** mon-fri noon-9pm, sat noon-8pm, sun noon-7pm
SUBWAY 6 to astor place, f, v to broadway/lafayette, n, r to 8th street

shopping   FOOD & DRINK   NIGHTLIFE   LODGING   CULTURE   various

In the 1960s, a steady stream of African students and immigrants flowed in and out of a small electrical store off London's Tottenham Court Road. Amazingly, they went there for the music. Stern's Electrical had what was, at the time, one of the only collections of African music in London, displayed behind shortwave radios, electrical fans and tea kettles. Eventually the electrical store closed, but a music store opened reviving the name of that once-pioneering shop. Over the decades, the store's fan base has grown, and now New Yorkers can enjoy one of the largest and most impressive collections of world music at this store near City Hall.

STERN'S MUSIC number 142, map E

ADDRESS 71 warren street, between west broadway and greenwich street **TELEPHONE** 212 964 5455 **WEBSITE** www.sternsmusicshop.com **OPENING HOURS** mon-sat 11am-9pm, sun 11am-7pm **SUBWAY** 2, 3 to park place

shopping   food & drink   nightlife   lodging   culture   various

SMOKE
number 143, map A

ADDRESS 2751 broadway, between 105th and 106th streets **TELEPHONE** 212 864 6662 **WEBSITE** www.smokejazz.com **OPENING HOURS** daily 5pm-4am **PRICE** fri-sat cover charge $15-$20 **SUBWAY** 1, 9 to 103rd street

There is absolutely no smoking allowed here – unless it's a smoking-good tune played on the Hammond B3. Exposed-brick walls, mahogany tables and deep-red velvet barstools and curtains give Smoke its authentic "cool cat" ambiance. And with just 70 seats, you'll have about as intimate a jazz/r&b/soul/latin experience as possible, short of hiring a band to play in your living room. There's no cover charge on weeknights, although patrons are encouraged to follow the minimum "$10-worth-of-drinks" rule; on Fridays and Saturdays anticipate a $20 cover charge. Either way, you're not likely to be disappointed with the caliber of music, the cocktails and what is one of New York's best-kept jazz secrets.

ADDRESS 288 lenox avenue (malcolm x boulevard), near 125th street **TELEPHONE** 212 427 0253 **WEBSITE** www.lenoxlounge.com **OPENING HOURS** mon-sun noon-4am **CREDIT CARDS** visa, mastercard, amex, diners club, discover **PRICE** average drink $5 **SUBWAY** 2, 3, a to 125th street

LENOX LOUNGE number 144, map A

Many Harlem locals, students, spiffsters and even a smattering of hipsters consider the Lenox Lounge the granddaddy of New York jazz clubs. Choose from the splendor of the recently renovated Art Deco front area, or head back to the Zebra Room, aptly named for its zebra-stripe wallpaper. It's here that you'll begin to get a sense of this lounge's legendary status. Have a seat, and take it all in, because you're on hallowed ground. Jazz legends Billie Holiday, Miles Davis, and John Coltrane all cut their teeth here. The food is good, but it's the legend surrounding the Lenox Lounge that makes it worth the trip uptown.

Sometimes you don't need to wander off the beaten path to find what you want. Take Birdland for example. Back in 1996, Birdland moved from 106th street in Harlem to the hustle and bustle of Times Square. If you're tired of cramped, uncomfortable jazz joints, but want quality music close by, you're in luck. Birdland (originally named in 1949 to honor jazz musician Charlie "Bird" Parker) is huge, with good sight lines, acoustics and a menu offering tried-and-true favorites from the Deep South. Top-notch jazz artists like Pat Metheny and Diana Krall have played here, as well as the big bands of Chico O'Farrill, Toshiko Akiyoshi and Maria Schneider.

number 145 map C # BIRDLAND

ADDRESS 315 west 44th street, between 8th and 9th avenues **TELEPHONE** 212 581 3080 **WEBSITE** www.birdlandjazz.com **OPENING HOURS** mon-sat 5pm-3am, sun noon-3am (first set 9pm, second set 11pm) **CREDIT CARDS** visa, mastercard, amex, discover **PRICE** music charge varies, $10 food/drink minimum per person at tables, one drink included with music charge at bar **SUBWAY** a, c, e to 42nd street

Thanks to Bowery Ballroom, the Lower East Side is home to one of the best music venues in the city. Built in 1929 on the foundation of an original theater, the building housed a jewelry store, a haberdashery, a shoe store and a carpet and lighting showroom before the current owners took it over in 1998. Watch mid-success bands, well-known local groups and even highly acclaimed indie rockers strut their stuff on the large, elevated stage. Views of the stage and sound quality are both very good. Bars exist on all three levels (including the exposed-stone basement), so a change of scenery is only a short walk away.

BOWERY BALLROOM number 146, map F

ADDRESS 6 delancey street, between bowery and chrystie streets **TELEPHONE** 212 533 2111 or 212 260 4700 **WEBSITE** www.boweryballroom.com **OPENING HOURS** call for show times **PRICE** $15-$25 **SUBWAY** j, m, z to delancey street

shopping | food & drink | nightlife | lodging | culture | various

number 147, map F # MERCURY LOUNGE

ADDRESS 217 east houston street, between ludlow and essex streets **TELEPHONE** 212 260 4700 **WEBSITE** www.mercuryloungenyc.com **OPENING HOURS** daily 6pm-4am **CREDIT CARDS** none **PRICE** $8-$15
SUBWAY f to 2nd avenue

The list of artists who have played the Mercury Lounge is bound to impress fans of modern (and not so modern) rock: Lou Reed, Joan Jett, Juliana Hatfield, They Might Be Giants, Radiohead, Squeeze, Luscious Jackson and even Tony Bennett. Between 1933 and 1993, the Mercury Lounge storefront housed a tombstone seller. Remnants of the operation have been incorporated into the scenery, including an embedded tombstone in the bar. But music is what the lounge does best, providing clean, crisp acoustics, good views (when you're standing) and an interesting mix of popular and unknown local bands, plus a bevy of touring alternative/indie rock and punk bands.

ADDRESS 237 west 42nd street **TELEPHONE** 212 997 4144 **WEBSITE** www.bbkingblues.com **OPENING HOURS** daily 11-2am **CREDIT CARDS** visa, mastercard, amex, diners club, discover **PRICE** $17 **SUBWAY** 1, 2, 3, 7, 9, a, c, e, n, r, s to 42nd street/times square

BB KING'S number 148, map C

Aside from excellent late-night blues, jazz, pop, rock and even zydeco, BB King's offers a religious experience every Sunday – the "Gospel Brunch." If you can't go uptown to Harlem, uptown comes to midtown, and it's as yummy as it is uplifting. The all-you-can-eat soul food buffet, featuring the temptations of heart-stopping (literally and figuratively speaking) smothered collard greens, southern-fried chicken and fried catfish is topped off with a healthy dose of redemption from the Harlem Gospel Choir. No dry sermons here, just toe-tapping, hand-clapping gospel tunes. This is one religious experience you won't regret dragging yourself out of bed for on a Sunday morning.

The Knitting Factory has been a venue for cutting-edge music, poetry, photography and video since 1994. On any given night, you can almost always catch a local or touring indie band in the main performance space, with smaller shows, videos and readings in the more intimate offshoot spaces – the Old Office and the KnitActive Sound Stage. In its current incarnation, the "Knit" covers four floors (with four bars, filled with the requisite black-clad, angst-ridden hipsters and artists) and should give you a good sense of the breadth of the art scene in New York City.

number 149, map E

KNITTING FACTORY

ADDRESS 74 leonard street, between broadway and church street **TELEPHONE** 212 219 3132 **WEBSITE** www.knittingfactory.com **OPENING HOURS** daily 5pm-4am **CREDIT CARDS** visa, mastercard, amex **PRICE** $5-$15 **SUBWAY** 6, j, m, n, r, q, w, z to canal street

Built in 1883, this was New York's tallest building until 1902. In 1905, the Chelsea became a hotel, and some of the 20th century's biggest names have either stayed or lived here, including Mark Twain, O. Henry, Dylan Thomas, Arthur Miller, Andy Warhol, William S. Burroughs, Willem de Kooning, Jackson Pollock, Sid Vicious and Janis Joplin. Original, elaborate architectural details remain, including the unique iron staircase. If you're not spending the night, stop in at the El Quijote Spanish restaurant off the lobby for some retro-1950s ambiance and cocktails at great prices. If you're A-list material, check out Serena Bar and Lounge, the hot spot in the basement.

ADDRESS 222 west 23rd street **TELEPHONE** 212 243 3700 **WEBSITE** www.hotelchelsea.com **CREDIT CARDS** visa, mastercard, amex **PRICE** $175–$300 **SUBWAY** 1, 9 to 23rd street

HOTEL CHELSEA   number 150, map C

shopping food & drink nightlife lodging culture various

SOB'S

number 151, map E

ADDRESS 204 varick street, at houston street **TELEPHONE** 212 243 4940 **WEBSITE** www.sobs.com **OPENING HOURS** mon-sat 6.30pm-4am **CREDIT CARDS** visa, mastercard, amex, diners club, discover **PRICE** average drink $8 **SUBWAY** 1, 9 to houston street

The Sounds of Brazil are not the only type of music you'll hear at SOB's. The musical lineup also features African, French Caribbean/Haitian, Latin alternative, salsa, reggae, urban and even a smattering of bhangra (a very hip, urban-Indian music style) in the basement. SOB's world music is further enhanced by a world kitchen, serving up delicious dishes of Latin and Brazilian origins and topping them off with a healthy selection of tropical drinks of the fruity, exotic bent. Considering the bamboo and palms interior setting and the dance-till-you-drop atmosphere, a stop at SOB's is like taking a quick jaunt to Latin America without leaving New York City!

ADDRESS 1 columbus circle **TELEPHONE** 212 258 9800 **WEBSITE** www.jazzatlincolncenter.org
OPENING HOURS tba **CREDIT CARDS** tba **PRICE** tba **SUBWAY** 1, 9, a, b, c, d to 59th street/columbus circle

JAZZ AT LINCOLN CENTER number 152, map C

OPEN OCTOBER 2004 In some ways, the opening of the new Jazz at Lincoln Center inside the monstrous and much-hyped AOL/Time Warner Center signifies a new era in jazz – a more commercial era, perhaps. In addition to the 100,000 square-foot Rose Hall, the center will feature Dizzy's Club Coca-Cola and the Allan Room, which have all been "engineered" for warmth and clarity of sound. The state-of-the-art facility will also house the Jazz Hall of Fame and projection screens and audio components designed to provide visitors with insight into the history of jazz. It will definitely be worth a visit, at least to get a sense of jazz, its past and its future.

shopping   food & drink   nightlife   lodging   culture   various

Without the Apollo Theater, the world might have had to live without the talents of performers like Ella Fitzgerald, Sarah Vaughan, James Brown, Billie Holiday, Ben E. King, Michael Jackson, Luther Vandross and Lauryn Hill. They all got their start at the world-famous "Amateur Night at the Apollo," a Wednesday night affair that has been launching young careers since 1934. The theater is a piece of Harlem history and continues to be a vital part of the community. Check the calendar to see what exciting events are planned.

number 153, map A **APOLLO THEATER**

ADDRESS 253 west 125th street, between adam clayton powell and frederick douglass boulevards
TELEPHONE 212 531 5305 **WEBSITE** www.apollotheater.com **OPENING HOURS** (box office) mon-tue, thu-fri 10am-6pm, wed 10am-8.30pm, sat noon-6pm **SUBWAY** 2, 3, a, b, c, d to 125th street

Industrialist-turned-philanthropist Andrew Carnegie opened Carnegie Hall in 1890, and since then it's been one of the world's most renowned venues for soloists, conductors and ensembles. It's also played home to important jazz events, historic lectures (including Winston Churchill, who delivered a speech here), noted educational forums and even a concert by the Beatles. The design of Carnegie Hall's main auditorium features a striking curvilinear shape, which allows the stage to become a focal point for five levels of seating. In fact, the acoustics are so good some have even claimed that the hall itself is an instrument! It's every classical musician's dream to play here... Come see why.

ADDRESS 881 7th avenue at 57th street **TELEPHONE** 212 247 7800 **WEBSITE** www.carnegiehall.org
OPENING HOURS mon-sat 11am-6pm, sun noon-6pm **SUBWAY** n, q, r, w to 57th street

CARNEGIE HALL number 154, map C

number 155, map C

TURNTABLES ON THE HUDSON

ADDRESS the frying pan, pier 63, 23rd street at west side highway **TELEPHONE** 212 560 5593 **WEBSITE** www.turntablesonthehudson.com **OPENING HOURS** fri 10pm-4am **PRICE** $10 **SUBWAY** n, q, r, w to 57th street

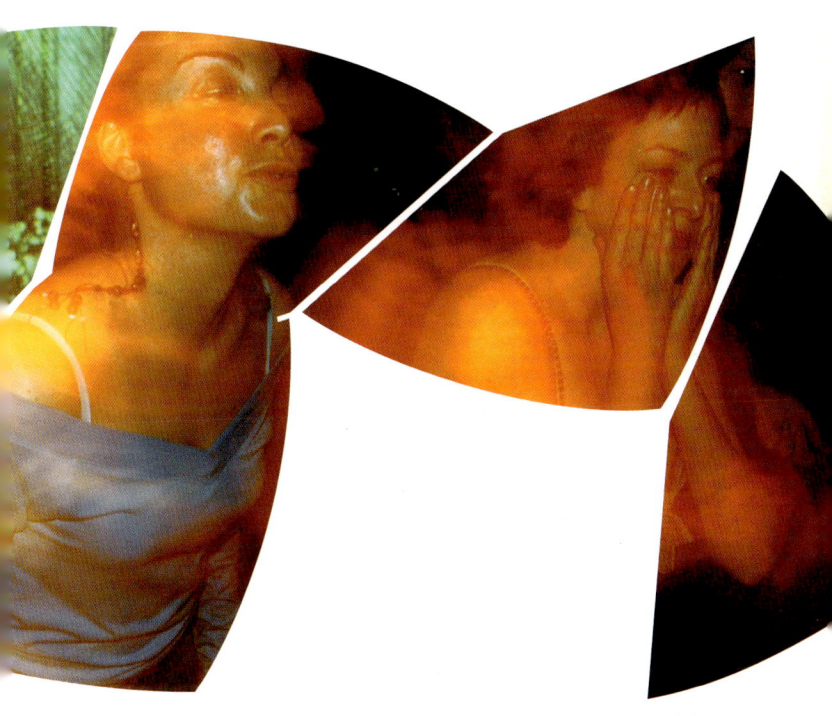

For the past five years, DJs Nickodemus and Mariano have been hosting one of the city's most unique underground dance parties. The parties usually take place on Friday nights in the Frying Pan, a decommissioned boat docked against Pier 63 in the Hudson River, or on the pier itself. The crowd doesn't stop grooving to the mix of house, hip-hop, dub, funk and jazz, heavily infused with world rhythms. Guest DJs, including Osiris, Jeannie Hopper and Nappy G., mix it up with their own sets and occasionally with live percussion. You can even take the TOTH vibe home with you: Nickodemus and Mariano have released several albums, available on the Web or at record stores in New York.

shopping   food & drink   nightlife   lodging   culture   variou

BODY & SOUL

shopping | food & drink | nightlife | lodging | culture | various

PAMPER YOURSELF

New York is a **crowded**, noisy and **dirty city**. Millions of people live within a few square miles of each other, constantly competing for the same scant resources, fighting over the same piece of smoked salmon at Zabar's, angling for the last seat on the Times Square shuttle at rush hour or drawing blood over a tiny one-room apartment on the Upper East Side. It's little wonder then that New Yorkers have to keep discovering (or inventing) new and **interesting ways** to **unwind**.

Everybody relaxes in a different way. Athletic types hit the swimming pool or squash court to work their frustrations out in beads of sweat. **Hedonists** melt their troubles away in a sauna or bathhouse. Shopaholics head for the stores to exercise their credit cards, and escapists find the best way to decompress is to **flee the city** completely.

Central Park is a nice place to go to **escape the pressures** of the city without actually leaving it. It's beautiful in all seasons and particularly nice in the off-season, when it is less crowded and more serene. Facilities are available for tennis, boating, biking, roller-blading and countless other physical activities. It's also a lovely place for a walk or to **lie down** in the sun. In the summer, there are **outdoor concerts**, street performers, baseball games and endless activities for kids and adults alike. In winter, what could be more romantic than skating at Wollman Rink and taking a ride in a horse-drawn carriage? The park is **the city's backyard**, and best of all: It's free!

The **riverfronts** on both the eastern and western fringes of the city are also **being revitalized** to accommodate residents and their active lifestyles. On the West Side, it's possible to follow a bike path from Battery Park at the southernmost tip of the island to 135th Street in Harlem, riding alongside the Hudson River almost all the way.

Riverside Park, which runs along the Hudson River north of 72nd Street, is a **verdant and vibrant** park in the summer and is home to a popular outdoor bar, several baseball fields and tennis courts, a marina, a skating park and even a beach volleyball court. Brooklyn is home to the lovely **Prospect Park**, as well as the **beaches** of Coney Island and Brighton. To really experience the seaside, however, New Yorkers take a trip to the Hamptons in Long Island or "the shore" in New Jersey.

For more **meditative forms of relaxation**, the city offers dozens of spas and yoga studios to choose from. Spas are the newest trend, and there seems to be one on every block. Each tries to outdo the competition by using more **exotic ingredients and methods** to massage, exfoliate, cleanse and hydrate you into a **state of bliss**.

To truly **achieve nirvana** however, many New Yorkers have delved into the study of yoga. There are hundreds of studios to choose from, and each has its own particular **vibe and atmosphere**. Some adhere to traditional Indian yogic traditions and are very simple, spiritual affairs. Others have all the flash of a Hollywood movie premiere and are **trendy, hip hangouts**. Choose whichever suits your needs the best, and you are sure to enjoy your experience.

There are plenty of **healthy eating** options in New York as well. Health food stores with organic ingredients abound, as do stores selling vitamins, nutritional supplements and farm fresh produce and restaurants serving healthy, **vegetarian** food.

If you're seeking a **higher spiritual calling**, you might just find your "satori" in New York. This is certainly the city to try your hand at many different traditions. Where else but New York could you experience Wicca, **Kabala**, Santeria, Sufism, Paganism and **Shamanism** in one day?

BODY & SOUL

shopping food & drink nightlife lodging culture various

SEE PAGE 206-213 FOR A MAP WITH ALL THE ADDRESSES FROM THIS GUIDE
(turn map 90°)

ADDRESS 240 east 53rd street, between 2nd and 3rd avenues **TELEPHONE** 212 758 5521 **WEBSITE** www.theosophy-ny.org/quest_bookshop.htm **OPENING HOURS** mon-fri 11am-8pm, sat noon-8pm, sun 1pm-6pm **CREDIT CARDS** visa, mastercard, amex **SUBWAY** 6, e, v to 51st street/lexington avenue

QUEST BOOKSHOP number 162, map D

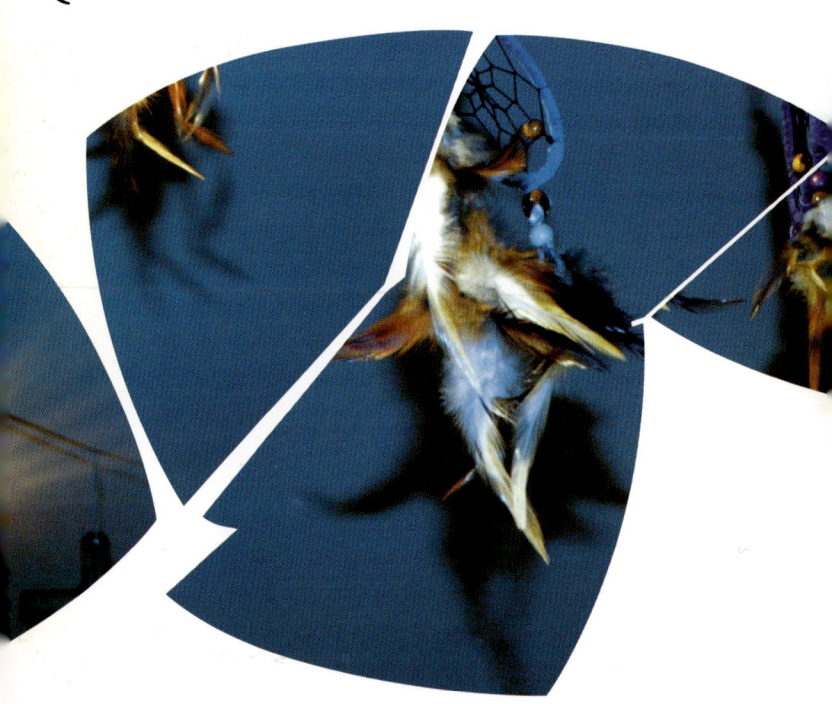

Spiritual seekers may quench their thirst for knowledge at this bookstore, run by the New York Theosophical Society. The organization was founded in New York in 1875 to "investigate the nature of the universe and humanity's place in it, to promote understanding of other cultures, and to be a nucleus of universal brotherhood among all human beings." Books at this small and unassuming store expand on theosophy, as well as many other ideas – in fact, the store covers everything from A (Astronomy) to Z (Zoroastrianism). Lectures, classes and workshops are also available for those who yearn to expand the boundaries of their universe.

shopping | food & drink | nightlife | lodging | culture | various

Lafco New York is the official American importer of the highly prized Santa Maria Novella cosmetic and bath products, originally made by monks in 13th-century Florence. Celebrities have favored these products ever since the time of Catherine de Medici. In fact, she had a fragrance personally crafted for her – "Water of the Queen," a blend of orange blossom and bergamot given to her at the time of her wedding to England's Henry II. The beautifully packaged products, still manufactured in Florence, are lovely to display, as well as pamper your body with. Other bath and beauty products are available, as are selected furniture and home decorations.

number 163, map E **LAFCO NEW YORK**

ADDRESS 285 lafayette street, between houston and prince streets **TELEPHONE** 212 925 0001 or 800 362 3677 **WEBSITE** www.lafcony.com **OPENING HOURS** tue-sat 11am-7pm, sun noon-7pm **SUBWAY** a, c, e to canal street

shopping | food & drink | nightlife | lodging | culture | variou

Shu Uemura, Japan's pioneering male makeup artist, opened his first store in Tokyo in 1983. He now has 200 stores in more than 20 countries, including this flagship New York beauty boutique, perfectly set in a trendy SoHo ironstone building. Uemura elevates makeup to an art form, but still makes it accessible for all. Get up close and personal with the line of products as you select the perfect tone for your complexion and see what your makeup will look like in a variety of light settings. There are also hundreds of brushes and other makeup tools from which to choose, including an eyelash curler that has its own cult following.

ADDRESS 121 greene street, between houston and prince streets **TELEPHONE** 212 979 5500 **WEBSITE** www.shu-uemura.com **CREDIT CARDS** visa, mastercard, amex **SUBWAY** f, s, v to broadway-lafayette; n, r to prince

SHU UEMURA number 164, map E

number 165, map E

BELL BATES NATURAL FOODS

ADDRESS 97 reade street, between west broadway and church street **TELEPHONE** 212 267 4300 **WEBSITE** www.bellbates.com **OPENING HOURS** mon-fri 9am-7pm, sat 10am-6pm **CREDIT CARDS** visa, mastercard, amex, diners club **SUBWAY** 1, 2, 3, 9 to chambers street

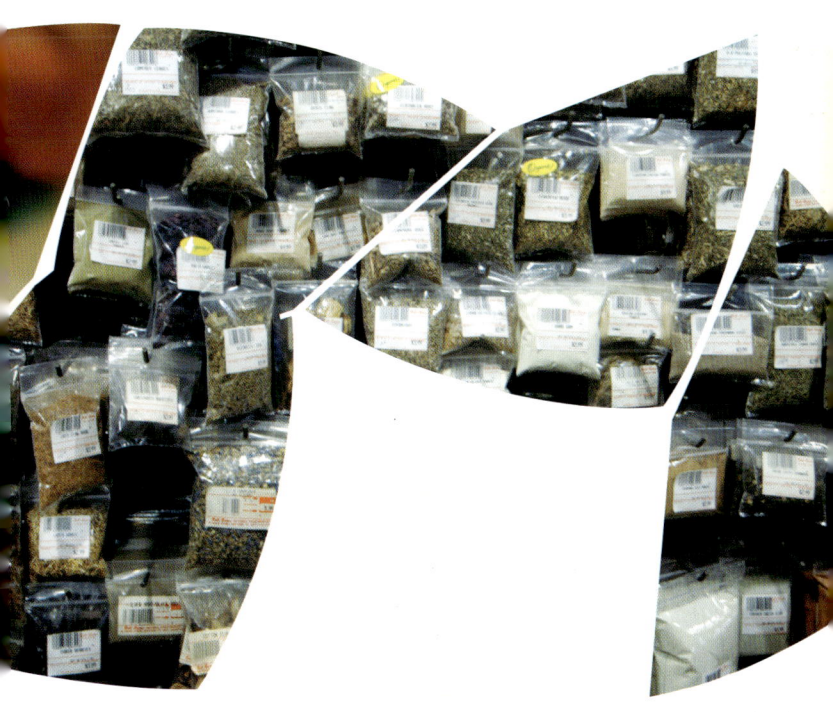

New York's largest health food emporium is also one of its favorites. This huge store, family-owned and operated for more than 100 years, offers everything to treat your body right. Grab a snack at the deli counter, or order a healthy, organic juice drink to recharge your batteries or help fight off an oncoming cold. All the fruits and vegetables sold in the store are carefully picked and guaranteed organic – meaning they haven't been sprayed with pesticides or herbicides and haven't been given any synthetic fertilizers. This is a good place to stock up on vitamins, herbs and spices, coffees and dietary supplements.

ADDRESS 152 allen street, near rivington street **TELEPHONE** 212 254 6512 or 866 59-VEGAN (toll-free)
WEBSITE www.mooshoes.com **OPENING HOURS** mon-sat 11.30am-7.30pm, sun noon-6pm
SUBWAY f to 2nd avenue

MOO SHOES number 166, map F

Vegans can be style-conscious as well as concerned citizens. Highly frustrated when they couldn't find a good-looking, non-leather pair of shoes, sisters Sara and Erica Kubersky eventually decided the only thing to do was start their own leather-free store. Selling shoes, bags, wallets, t-shirts and other accessories, the store has now also become a resource for cruelty-free and animal-friendly activities, including animal adoption days and book signings. The sisters themselves are a wealth of information on leather alternatives and the vegan lifestyle.

shopping   food & drink   nightlife   lodging   culture   various

You might think downtowners care more about their health than uptowners, given the locations of the largest and best health food stores. Wholesome Market, a mega health food store that stocks everything you need for a macrobiotic, vegan or other health-oriented lifestyle, has two locations, and both are south of 14th Street! With the help of this store, both you and your pet can adhere to a healthy meal plan. You'll also find everything you need to organically cleanse your skin, body and even your house.

number 167, map E   # WHOLESOME MARKET

ADDRESS (1) 489 broome street, at west broadway (2) 93 university place, between 11th and 12th streets
TELEPHONE (1) 212 431 7434 (2) 212 353 3663 **OPENING HOURS** mon-sat 7am-9.30pm, sun 8am-9.30pm
SUBWAY (1) 6 to prince street (2) 4, 5, 6, l, n, q, r, w to 14th street/union square

shopping   FOOD & DRINK   NIGHTLIFE   LODGING   CULTURE   various

You may be tempted to close your eyes and meditate as you enter Tao and see the focal point of the décor: a giant, floating Buddha hovering over a serene reflecting pool. But don't tune out too much, or you're liable to miss this unbeatable dining experience. The mystical surroundings are just the beginning – Tao's chefs are masters in their traditions and serve up Thai, Japanese and Hong Kong Chinese specialties. Come in just for drinks if you can't make it for dinner. The Love Potion #9 tantalizingly offers "Tao Lifeforce Energy Potion" as one of its ingredients.

ADDRESS 42 east 58th street, at madison avenue **TELEPHONE** 212 888 2288 **WEBSITE** www.taorestaurant.com **OPENING HOURS** mon-tue 11.30am-midnight, wed-fri 11.30-1am, sat 5pm-1am, sun 5pm-midnight **CREDIT CARDS** visa, mastercard, amex, diners club **PRICE** $20 **SUBWAY** 4, 5, 6 to lexington avenue, n, r to 59th street

TAO
number 168, map C

number 169 map C, E ## ZEN PALATE

ADDRESS (1) 663 9th avenue, at 46th street (2) 34 union square east, at 16th street (3) 2170 broadway, at 76th street **TELEPHONE** (1) 212 582 1669 (2) 212 614 9291 (3) 212 501 7768 **WEBSITE** www.zenpalate.com **OPENING HOURS** (1) daily 11.30am-11pm (2) daily 11.30am-3pm, 5.30-10.30pm (3) sun-thu noon-10.30pm, fri-sat 11am-11pm **PRICE** $15 **CREDIT CARDS** visa, mastercard, amex, diners club, discover **SUBWAY** (1) a, c, e to 42nd street (2) 4, 5, 6, l, n, q, r, w to 14th street/union square (3) 1, 9 to 79th street

Eating food this healthy and wholesome must earn points towards nirvana, right? Well, even if it doesn't, it can't hurt to eat a meal at one of Zen Palate's three Manhattan locations. The food is fresh, healthy, Asian-inspired and all vegetarian. The Union Square location is trendy and always busy – especially at the outdoor café, which fills with a young, hip and laid back crowd. The food ranges from the familiar (spring rolls and noodle soups) to exotic (Mexican-style moo-shu). No alcohol is served, but your meal will make you feel so virtuous that a drink could only induce guilt.

shopping   food & drink   nightlife   lodging   culture   various

ADDRESS (1) 300 amsterdam avenue, at 74th street (2) 565 3rd avenue, at 37th street **TELEPHONE** (1) 212 769 1212 (2) 212 490 1558 **OPENING HOURS** mon-wed noon-11pm, thu-fri noon-midnight, sat 11.30am-midnight, sun 11am-10pm **PRICE** $14 **CREDIT CARDS** visa, mastercard, amex **SUBWAY** (1) 1, 2, 3, 9 to 72nd street (2) 6 to 33rd street

JOSIE'S number 170, map C, D

Josie's, a very popular Upper West Side restaurant serving mostly dairy-free and organic meals, is conveniently located close to Crunch, a trendy health club. This might account for the ever-present crowds lapping up wheatgrass and soy drinks. But it's not just fitness junkies who fill this California-style restaurant and its newer Murray Hill location. Vegetarians will love the dairy-free pizzas and veggie burgers, and meat eaters will be pleased to know that they can eat farm-raised or free-range sausages, steaks and chickens with a clear conscience. The brightly colored atmosphere, cramped tables and glassed-in sidewalk café are warm and inviting.

shopping   food & drink   nightlife   lodging   culture   various

Long before this corner of SoHo became one of the most fashionable addresses in the city and "certified organic" rolled off everyone's tongue, there was Spring Street Natural. The restaurant was founded in 1973 and moved to this large, airy corner location in 1985. The philosophy has remained the same over the years: to serve whole, natural, minimally processed foods using as many natural ingredients as possible. The interior space is as organic as the food, with simple, minimal decorations and loads of natural sunlight. Although there are a number of vegan and macrobiotic options, there are also innovative seafood and poultry options for the carnivore.

number 171, map E

SPRING STREET NATURAL

ADDRESS 62 spring street, at lafayette street **TELEPHONE** 212 966 0290 **WEBSITE** www.springstreetnatural.com **OPENING HOURS** sun-thu 11.30am-11.30pm, fri-sat 11.30-1am **PRICE** $12 **CREDIT CARDS** visa, mastercard, amex **SUBWAY** 6 to spring street, n, r to prince street

Following the Asian principles of yin and yang, HanGawi serves vegetarian Korean meals that are in perfect balance. In order to achieve good health, the restaurant's owners believe that a diet needs to consist of a balance of green vegetables and fruits, roots, radishes, potatoes and carrots. If this sounds complicated, select the Emperor's Meal, a tasty selection of starters, appetizers, entrée and dessert, and let HanGawi worry about the details. This is considered one of the best vegetarian dining experiences in the city.

ADDRESS 12 east 32nd street, between 5th and madison avenues **TELEPHONE** 212 213 0077 **WEBSITE** www.hangawirestaurant.com **OPENING HOURS** (lunch) mon-fri noon-3pm, sat-sun 1-5pm (dinner) mon-thu 5-10.30pm, fri-sat 5-11pm, sun 5-10pm **CREDIT CARDS** visa, mastercard, amex, diners club **PRICE** $17, emperor's meal $30 **SUBWAY** 6 to 33rd street, n, r to 28th street

HANGAWI   number 172, map C

shopping   food & drink   **nightlife**   lodging   culture   various

ADDRESS 110 rivington street, between ludlow and essex streets **TELEPHONE** 212 614 2494 **OPENING HOURS** mon-sat 5pm-4am **CREDIT CARDS** visa, mastercard, amex, diners club **PRICE** $8 **SUBWAY** f, v, to lower east side/2nd avenue

number 173, map F   # VERLAINE

Paul Verlaine was a French poet who, together with two friends, started a movement called the Decadents. Their guiding philosophy stated that only self is important and that poetry is a method of preserving extreme experiences of the senses. Verlaine was basically a romantic and a drunk; who better to name a bar after? Occasional hedonism is good for the soul – so indulge your "self" at this plush, Vietnamese-inspired Lower East Side lounge. The food is interesting, the drinks are delicious and the crowd is almost always beautiful, if not always literary.

ADDRESS 299 madison avenue, at 41st street **TELEPHONE** 212 983 4500 **WEBSITE** www.libraryhotel.com
PRICE from $300, including breakfast **SUBWAY** 4, 5, 6, 7, s to 42nd street/grand central

LIBRARY HOTEL number 174, map C

A hotel organized by the Dewey Decimal System, the filing system used by libraries, doesn't sound like a spiritual sanctuary or vacation for the soul. In fact, it sounds like quite the opposite – but don't jump to conclusions. A room on the 12th floor, room 1200.001, is decorated with, inspired by and filled with books about Eastern Religion. You might get so caught up in your research that you forget to leave the hotel! Ask for soul-satisfying room 1100.006, the Love room, or any of the other 60 unique rooms at this small, remarkable midtown hotel located right near 5th Avenue, Bryant Park and Grand Central Station.

Whether you're interested in trying yoga for the first time or are already a practitioner and need a quick fix, Jivamukti is one of the best bets in the city. It's big, glamorous and dynamic. Beginners are advised to try the Basic Class, while those more familiar with "asanas" might feel more comfortable in an Open Class. The atmosphere, while conducive to yoga and relaxation, is also decidedly New York in its showiness; a large waterfall takes up an entire wall of the lobby, not to mention the gift store where you can pick up branded merchandise, including CDs for your home practice.

JIVAMUKTI
number 175, map D

ADDRESS (1) 404 lafayette street, between east 4th street and astor place (2) 853 lexington avenue, between 64th & 65th streets **TELEPHONE** (1) 212 353 0214 (2) 212 396 4200 **WEBSITE** www.jivamuktiyoga.com **OPENING HOURS** call for class schedules **SUBWAY** (1) 6 to astor place (2) 4, 5, 6, n, r to 59th street, 6 to 68th street, f to 63rd street

shopping   food & drink   nightlife   lodging   culture   variou[s]

Plan to spend your Sunday touring Harlem, one of the city's liveliest and most underrated neighborhoods. A Harlem Spirituals tour begins near Times Square and heads north into Harlem, leading you past some of the area's most famous landmarks. Your next stop will be at church, so be sure to dress appropriately. But fear not: This is no dull church service. You're in Harlem, so you can expect an afternoon filled with soul-uplifting, interactive gospel choir music. End your tour, if you so choose, with a more than satisfying Sunday "soul food" brunch.

ADDRESS tour begins at 690 8th avenue, between 43rd and 44th streets **TELEPHONE** 212 391 0900 **WEBSITE** harlemspirituals.com **OPENING HOURS** tour begins sun 9am (reservations are necessary) **PRICE** $45 **SUBWAY** 1, 2, 3, 7, 9, n, q, r, s, w to times square/42nd street

HARLEM SPIRITUALS   number 176, map C

shopping   food & drink   nightlife   lodging   culture   various

number 177, map E   **MAXIMUS SOHO**

ADDRESS 15 mercer street, between grand and canal streets **TELEPHONE** 212 431 3333 **WEBSITE** www.maximusspasalon.com **PRICE** water journey $85 **SUBWAY** a, c, e, n, r to canal street

This spa looks like a typical turn-of-the-century SoHo building from the outside, but inside it is state-of-the-art. Glass, chrome and steel blend elegantly with the building's original brick walls and columns. Take a "Maximus Water Journey," the spa's signature treatment. It's just what you need on a cold winter day or a humid, summer afternoon. It starts with a salt scrub to exfoliate your body, whisks you into a Swiss shower and then to a tub, where warm water jets melt away any remaining tension. You'll end up in a steam cabinet with water cascading over your back and finish by having your skin moisturized to perfection.

ADDRESS 7 east 14th street, between 5th avenue and union square west **TELEPHONE** 212 620 4329
WEBSITE www.acquabeautybar.com **OPENING HOURS** mon, thu 10am-9pm, tue, wed, fri 10am-8pm, sat, sun 10am-7pm **SUBWAY** 4, 5, 6, l, n, q, r, w to 14th street/union square

ACQUA BEAUTY BAR number 178, map C

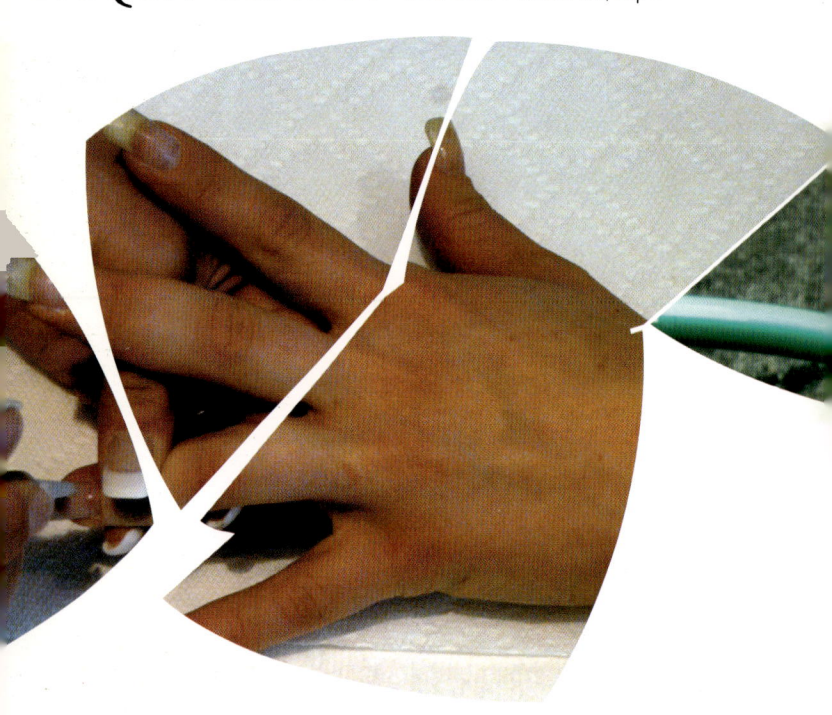

Join the hip crowd at their favorite "watering" hole. You can pamper yourself in first-class fashion with a beauty treatment at Acqua, which reportedly gives some of the best pedicures in town. Body massage choices include Chinese Tui Na, yoga-like Thai massage and a sensual Indonesian body treatment involving such things as a ground rice scrub, fragrant oil massage, vitamin-rich body masque and herbal compress. Acqua's guiding philosophy is that beauty is an expression of the balance between outer attractiveness and inner harmony. In other words: When you look good, you feel good.

shopping   food & drink   nightlife   lodging   culture   various

Biking is good for the body and the mind, especially in New York. No jostling down overcrowded sidewalks, dodging between tourists, shoppers and businessmen… With a bike you won't have to contend with maddening rush hour traffic or put your life in the hands of a cabbie with a one-way ticket to self-destruction. Instead, you can grab life by the handlebars and hit the open road on two wheels. Toga Bike Shop is ready when you are, with all the gear you'll need, including bike rentals. It's also conveniently located near the West Side Bike Path, which runs from the southern tip of Manhattan to 135th Street in Harlem.

number 179, map C **TOGA BIKE SHOP**

ADDRESS 110 west end avenue, at 64th street **TELEPHONE** 212 799 9625 **WEBSITE** www.togabikes.com
OPENING HOURS mon-fri 11am-7pm, sat 10am-6pm, sun 11am-5pm **PRICE** $30 for 24 hours (+$300 refundable deposit) **SUBWAY** 1, 9 to 66th street

shopping　　food & drink　　nightlife　　lodging　　culture　　various

NYC IN 20 STOPS

TAKE A BITE OUT OF THE BIG APPLE

New Yorkers are **highly opinionated people**, which makes it almost impossible to ever come to a consensus about any one thing, let alone "the best" of something.

New Yorkers are **fiercely proud** of their city. In fact, most of them say they would never dream of living anywhere else. This is ironic, since many of them moved to New York from somewhere else, but it doesn't take long for the city to get **under your skin**. You know you're truly a New Yorker when the thought of leaving the city – unless it's for a jet set vacation – seems like an odd and frankly unsavory thing to do.

New Yorkers are a very **passionate bunch of people**. They either love things or they hate them. There's very little room for negotiation with most New Yorkers. There's never a lack of something to review and people to review it, and if a particularly respected reviewer admits to hating something, you can be sure the place is as good as gone.

Your **top ten favorite places in the city** will likely be very different than someone else's, but one person's choice is certainly no better than another's. That is truly the beauty of New York: You can **make it your own**. Explore streets that aren't listed in guidebooks. Duck into local grocery and convenience stores just to see what kind of products they stock…

You'll get a **good sense** of the neighborhood this way. **Ride the subway** to a random stop, get off and walk around. Really experience the city, and you'll come away with more than a tourist's impression of it – You'll let it seep into your consciousness.

One good way to explore the city is to **strike up random conversations** with people. Ask a New Yorker on the subway where he most likes to eat Thai food, and you're liable to miss your stop because he'll fill you with **so much information**. Engage a shop clerk in conversation about where she bought her shoes, and you'll soon discover some offbeat and **fantastic** little places. This is good advice in any city, but especially in New York, where everyone has a point of view that they love to share.

The New York Press, a free weekly newspaper, publishes a yearly list of the city's "50 Most **Loathsome** New Yorkers," as judged by the readers themselves. Past lists included news anchormen, **criminals**, magazine editors, actors, **entrepreneurs** and several real estate developers. The newspaper's editors admitted they would need four or five "Top 50" lists to include all the loathed locals that are nominated to them.

shopping   food & drink   nightlife   lodging   culture   various

That's the kind of town this is. If there's any point to all this, it's simply to say that there's no such thing as the best of the city. The city is there in all its **gore** and all its **glory**, ripe for the taking and ready to be whatever you want it to be.

This chapter by no means represents the "best of" New York. There are dozens of other **landmarks** (some that are mentioned in other parts of this book, some that are not) that are crucial to any visitor's well-rounded **tour of the city**, just as there are scores of restaurants, shops and clubs that are definitely worth checking out.

The ultimate aim of this chapter is to capture some quintessentially New York experiences. With the **time-bound** traveler in mind, I've laid out stores that serve as **one-stop-shops**, restaurants that offer some of the best – or at least most unique – dining experiences in the city and sights that shouldn't be missed. Use these selections as a **guide** to getting a better **bite** out of the Big Apple. There are three hotels in this chapter.

NY IN 20 STOPS

SEE PAGE 206-213 FOR A MAP WITH ALL THE ADDRESSES FROM THIS GUIDE
(turn map 90°)

185

ADDRESS 60 wooster street, between spring and broome streets **TELEPHONE** 212 334 6354 **WEBSITE** www.stevenalan.com **OPENING HOURS** thu noon-8pm, fri-wed noon-7pm **CREDIT CARDS** visa, mastercard, amex **SUBWAY** n, r to prince street

STEVEN ALAN number 186, map E

The floors sag a bit, and the space seems too small for everything that's in it, but nevertheless this is one store that "fashionistas" won't want to miss. Steven Alan is known for carrying the hippest, most cutting-edge clothing from the hottest designers. In fact, he's even been called the "patron saint of fashion." Each season, the store features a new designer, while continuing to stock a wide range of options for men and women, including the store's own label, as well as bags, shoes, accessories and jewelry. The helpful, friendly staff provides a comfortable, no-pressure environment, and you're sure to walk out with something you love.

shopping | food & drink | nightlife | lodging | culture | various

Bendel's is a selective, ritzy and super-stylish department store. During the disco era, this was the place to get groovy gear, and the store still stocks young, hip favorites like Earl jeans, Shoshanna dresses and Richard Tyler evening wear. The cosmetics section on the ground floor is legendary, with brands such as Vincent Longo, Trish McEvoy, MAC and Bobbi Brown. Upstairs is a row of mini-boutiques including Agent Provocateur Lingerie, Flight 001 Travel Shop, Mary Quant, Rick Owens, Catherine Malandrino and Diane Von Furstenburg. Walk out with one of those brown-and-white striped bags, and you'll be recognized throughout New York as a shopper who's in the know.

number 187, map C **HENRI BENDEL**

ADDRESS 712 5th avenue, at 56th street **TELEPHONE** 212 247 1100 **OPENING HOURS** fri-wed 10am-7pm, thu 10am-8pm, sun noon-6pm **CREDIT CARDS** visa, mastercard, amex **SUBWAY** e, v to 5th avenue/53rd street

shopping   food & drink   nightlife   lodging   culture   various

Century 21 is a bargain hunter's heaven. Designer clothing is discounted 40 to 70 percent at this rambling store, although you have to be tough to find the great deals. The racks are a study in chaos, and when you find something good you'll probably also find several fashion vultures behind you. Contain your glee as you head to the dressing room, so they don't catch on to your incredible bargain. (Gents, there aren't any dressing rooms for you.) If you're looking for a specific item, you'll be highly frustrated, but if you're prowling for good clothes at good prices, you'll have to be dragged out of this theater of thrift.

ADDRESS 22 cortlandt street, at day street **TELEPHONE** 212 227 9092 **WEBSITE** www.c21stores.com **OPENING HOURS** mon-wed, fri 7.45am-8pm, thu 7.45am-8.30pm, sat 10am-8pm, sun 11am-7pm **CREDIT CARDS** visa, mastercard, amex, discover **SUBWAY** a, c to chambers street

CENTURY 21 number 188, map E

number 189, map B, D **SCOOP**

ADDRESS (1) 532 broadway, between prince and spring streets (2) 1275 3rd avenue, between 73rd and 74th streets **TELEPHONE** (1) 212 925 2886 (2) 212 535 5577 **WEBSITE** www.scoopnyc.com **OPENING HOURS** mon-sat 11am-8pm, sun 11am-7pm **SUBWAY** (1) 6 to spring street, n, r to prince street (2) 6 to 77th street

Scoop celebrates being a woman by stocking everything an "it" girl needs to look fabulous. Whatever the designer du jour, it's here, and it's in style. This is targeted shopping at its best, with great products, good prices and a groovy atmosphere. Whether you are in SoHo, on the Upper East Side or in the Hamptons, Scoop's prepared to provide you with your fashion fix. The racks are neatly organized by item, color, classification and trend, making this the perfect one-stop shop for the busy traveler.

ADDRESS 888 broadway, at 19th street TELEPHONE 212 473 3000 WEBSITE www.abchome.com OPENING HOURS mon-fri 10am-8pm, sat 10am-7pm, sun 11am-6.30pm CREDIT CARDS visa, mastercard, amex SUBWAY 6, n, r to 14th street/union square

ABC CARPET AND HOME

number 190, map C

ABC is huge – so huge that it takes two buildings to display all its wares. It's possible to spend the entire day browsing the selection of items, including Asian and European antiques and reproductions, modern designs, table linens, drapery, ethnic furniture, bath towels, bed sheets, jewelry, throw pillows... But wait, there's more! There are two restaurants (Lucy, serving upscale Mexican food, and Pipa, serving tapas and other Spanish favorites), a hair salon, an electronics boutique and a branch of the very popular Le Pain Quotidien Belgian bakery. 881 Broadway, across the street from the main store, has three floors of carpets and designer rugs.

Remember that scene in "When Harry Met Sally" where Meg Ryan fakes an orgasm? That was filmed at Katz's. Even though some New Yorkers argue that you can get a better corned beef sandwich elsewhere, you'd be hard pressed to find one who doesn't have a soft spot for Katz's. The restaurant was established in 1888, and sandwiches are still made on the premises and served either cafeteria-style or at your table. The sandwiches are so packed with meat that even half is hard to finish. Try warm pastrami on rye or a traditional Reuben, and you're on your way to becoming a true "New Yawker."

number 191, map F **KATZ'S DELI**

ADDRESS 205 east houston street, at ludlow street **TELEPHONE** 212 254 2246 **WEBSITE** www.katzdeli.com **OPENING HOURS** sun-tue 8am-10pm, wed-thu 8am-11pm, fri-sat 8-3am **CREDIT CARDS** visa, mastercard, amex **PRICE** $6 **SUBWAY** f, v to lower east side/2nd avenue

This underground restaurant, beneath the main floor of Grand Central Station, is one of the coolest locations in the city. Built in 1913 and renovated after a fire in 1997, the restaurant is an architectural and gastronomic wonder. The best seats are at the diner-style counters, and at lunchtime you can usually expect to wait for one. However, the incredible clam chowder and array of fresh, raw oysters (nearly 30 varieties) makes it well worth the wait. For those too impatient to stand around, reservations are accepted in the adjoining main dining room. This is truly a New York classic.

ADDRESS grand central lower concourse, enter 42nd street at lexington avenue **TELEPHONE** 212 490 6650 **WEBSITE** www.oysterbarny.com **OPENING HOURS** mon-fri 11.30am-9.30pm, sat 5.30-9.30pm **CREDIT CARDS** visa, mastercard, amex, diners club, discover **PRICE** $22 **SUBWAY** 4, 5, 6, 7, s to 42nd street/grand central

GRAND CENTRAL OYSTER BAR

number 192, map C

ADDRESS 42 east 20th street, between broadway and park avenue south **TELEPHONE** 212 477 0777 **WEBSITE** www.gramercytavern.com **OPENING HOURS** (lunch) mon-fri noon-2pm (dinner) sun-thu 5.30-10pm, fri-sat 5.30-11pm **CREDIT CARDS** visa, mastercard, amex, diners club, discover **PRICE** $25 **SUBWAY** 6, n, r, w to 23rd street

number 193, map C

GRAMERCY TAVERN

Gramercy Tavern has a reputation amongst aficionados as being one of the best restaurants in New York. The service is impeccable, the seasonal menu of creative dishes never disappoints, the wine list is brilliantly chosen, and the ambiance is warm, comfortable and not overbearing. If this sounds like the kind of place you'd be interested in, be sure to book a reservation well in advance. New Yorkers wait for weeks for these prized seats – at least that gives them time to save some money and lose some weight in preparation for the feast. Those on a limited budget could try coming for lunch and choosing the three-course market menu.

ADDRESS 86 bedford street, between bleecker street and 7th avenue **TELEPHONE** 212 675 4449
OPENING HOURS sun-thu 5pm-midnight, fri-sat 5pm-2am **CREDIT CARDS** visa, mastercard, amex **PRICE** $6
SUBWAY 1, 9 to christopher street/sheridan square

CHUMLEY'S number 194, map E

Chumley's is a slice of history. Located on one of the earliest recorded streets in New York, it's old, creaky, cozy and comfortable. The pub started in 1928 and was famous as a literary hangout for people like F. Scott Fitzgerald (who had his wedding reception here), Orson Welles (who supposedly wrote "Citizen Kane" at one of the wooden tables), John Steinbeck and William Faulkner. The walls are still covered with book jackets from famous former patrons. There are no signs outside the pub, in tribute to its history as a speakeasy during Prohibition. (Look for the two secret entrances.) Once you find it, however, you won't want to leave.

The Upper "Ouest" Side has become fertile ground for stylish French bistros featuring celebrity chefs, and Aix is no exception. Chef Didier Virot, a protégé of popular restaurateur Jean-Georges Vongerichten, produces inventive twists on Provencal dishes in this warm, comfortable bi-level space, offering choices such as tuna marinated with cucumber and coriander, served with sheep's milk yogurt horseradish sauce, or venison roasted with quince and chestnut, served with a celery coconut puree and spiced cassis sauce. Be sure to leave room for desserts such as rosemary apple brioche and chocolate banana tart, elegantly crafted by pastry chef Jehangir Mehta.

number 195, map A **AIX**

ADDRESS 2398 broadway, at 88th street **TELEPHONE** 212 874 7400 **WEBSITE** www.aixnyc.com **OPENING HOURS** sun-thu 5.30-10.30pm, fri-sat 5.30-11pm **CREDIT CARDS** visa, mastercard, amex **PRICE** $28 **SUBWAY** 1, 9 to 86th street

shopping   Food & Drink   nightlife   Lodging   culture   various

Enter through the Village Yokocho Japanese restaurant, and head upstairs to the second floor, then pass through the curtains for the tiny Angel's Share. Inside, a Japanese bartender will mix your cocktail with precision and reverence. Angel's Share is so quirky, so clandestine, so perfectly contrived that it's an absolute must-see. How many other bars can you think of that have signs explicitly ordering guests not to stand, shout or come in groups of more than four? Try a sake cocktail or other Asian-influenced drink and snack on sashimi, dim sum and fried oysters. You'll feel so plugged in – lots of New Yorkers don't even know about this place!

ADDRESS 8 stuyvesant street, between 2nd and 3rd avenues **TELEPHONE** 212 777 5415 **OPENING HOURS** daily 7pm-2.30am **PRICE** average drink $8 **SUBWAY** 6 to astor place, n, r, w to 8th street/NYU

ANGEL'S SHARE   number 196, map F

number 197, map C # HOWARD JOHNSON'S

ADDRESS 1551 broadway, at 46th street **TELEPHONE** 212 354 1445 **OPENING HOURS** sun-thu 7-2.30am, fri-sat 7-3.45am **CREDIT CARDS** visa, mastercard, amex **PRICE** $10 **SUBWAY** 2, 3, 9, a, c, e to 42nd street/times square

In the middle of Times Square is a relic that cannot be missed. Howard Johnson's is an extravaganza of vinyl, Formica and chrome – diner décor straight out of the 1950s. The waiters and waitresses look like they might have reached their primes in the 50s too, but they are miles more efficient than the actors and actresses that serve you in more upscale restaurants. Dining here must be done with tongue planted firmly in cheek – come for the experience, not the "haute cuisine." That said, you can get a perfectly decent burger or fries with gravy, and nothing is groovier than Happy Hour in the cocktail lounge.

ADDRESS 221 2nd avenue, between 13th and 14th streets **TELEPHONE** 212 677 3161
WEBSITE www.secondhome.citysearch.com **PRICE** from $75

SECOND HOME ON SECOND AVENUE number 198, map D

Carlos Delfin's guesthouse, Second Home on Second Avenue, is literally what it sounds like. Seven cozy rooms are tastefully but subtly decorated with themes like Peruvian, tribal, Caribbean or 20th-century modern (note: only two of them have private bathrooms), and the accommodations are clean, sparse and very private. You'll have access to a shared kitchen so you can go shopping at the nearby Union Square farmer's market, make your dinner to order and then head out for a night in one of many neighborhood bars. It's like having your own pied-a-terre in the city without having to pay crazy New York rents. What a deal!

60 Thompson is loaded with laid-back charm. From the pleasant sidewalk patio and trendy Thom restaurant on the street level to the cool second-floor lobby bar and guests-only rooftop terrace, the hotel is a serene oasis in SoHo. The 100 guest rooms are beautifully decorated with paneled leather walls, dark wood headboards and crisp Frette linen sheets on the beds. The whole experience is understated and elegant – a touch of class in an otherwise brazen neighborhood. The duplex penthouse suite is for real high rollers and features a fireplace, private roof deck with views in three directions and a wall of windows.

number 199, map E **60 THOMPSON**

ADDRESS 60 thompson, between spring and broome streets **TELEPHONE** 877 431 0400 **WEBSITE** www.60thompson.com **CREDIT CARDS** visa, mastercard, amex **PRICE** from $350 **SUBWAY** c, e to spring street

This chic hotel is one of New York's newest and best-kept secrets. The maritime theme is carried out through the use of deep blues and greens, wood-paneled walls that resemble a ship's stateroom and unique porthole windows that actually open. This is the only boutique hotel you'll find in this part of Chelsea, and the prices are still reasonable for the style you get. The hotel's restaurants attract a young, hip crowd, and the proximity to trendy eateries, bars and stores in the Meat Packing District and the West Village is a huge attraction.

ADDRESS 363 west 16th street at 9th avenue **TELEPHONE** 212 242 4300 **WEBSITE** www.themaritimehotel.com
CREDIT CARDS visa, mastercard, amex **PRICE** from $140 **SUBWAY** 1, 9 to 18th street, a, c, e, to 14th street

THE MARITIME HOTEL number 200, map C

ADDRESS 1000 5th avenue, between 80th and 83rd streets **TELEPHONE** 212 535 7710 **WEBSITE** www.metmuseum.org **OPENING HOURS** tue-thu 9.30am-5.30pm, fri-sat 9.30am-9pm **PRICE** suggested donation $12 **SUBWAY** 6 to 77th street

number 201, map A # METROPOLITAN MUSEUM

The Metropolitan is ranked amongst the world's finest museums; to come to New York and miss it would be sacrilege. The museum's imposing structure evokes the palace at Versailles, and the collection inside takes your breath away. If you're pressed for time, at least visit the exquisite collection of Egyptian artifacts and the Temple of Dendur, which was given to the United States by Egypt and installed in the Met block by block. Other collections include Greek and Roman art, Drawings and Prints, the Costume Institute, Islamic Art, Arms and Armor... too many to list! Be sure to set aside some time: This is a "must see."

ADDRESS 945 madison avenue, at 75th street **TELEPHONE** 212 570 3641 **WEBSITE** www.whitney.org
OPENING HOURS wed-thu, sat-sun 11am-6pm, fri 1-9pm **PRICE** $12 **SUBWAY** 6 to 77th street

WHITNEY MUSEUM number 202, map A

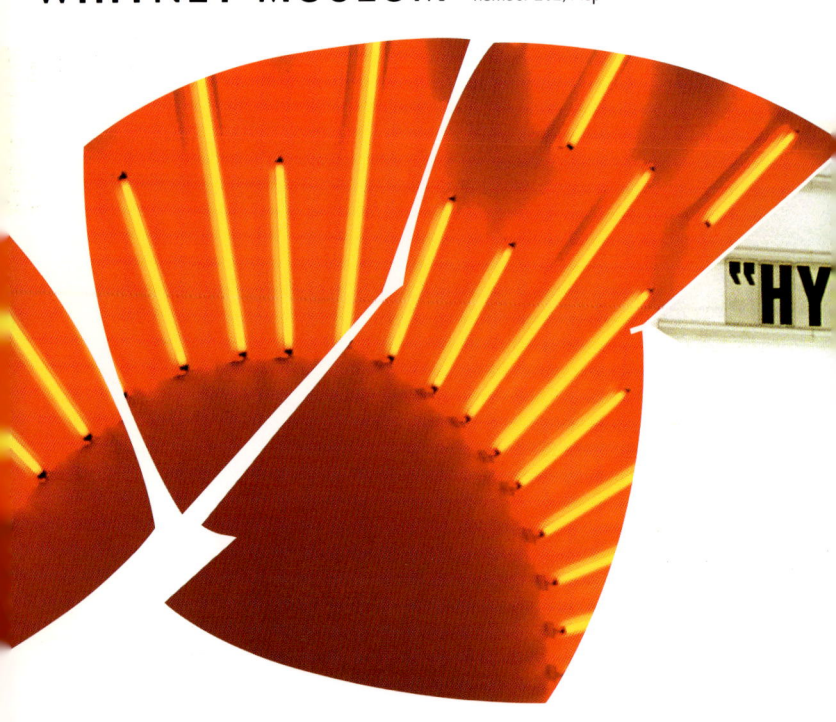

Explore 20th and 21st century American art at the Upper East Side's Whitney Museum. From Jasper Johns, Andy Warhol, Alexander Calder and Kiki Smith to quilts, crafts and video installations by unknown artists, the Whitney is an exploration of American artistic expression. Every year since 1932 the museum has held the internationally known Biennial, a survey of contemporary aesthetic trends and developments. The original museum was founded in 1931 and moved to this brown, stepped building designed by architect Marcel Breuer in 1966.

shopping　　　food & drink　　　nightlife　　　lodging　　　culture　　　various

The Film Forum is a quirky repertory cinema with a devoted following. From Fellini to Fassbinder, this is the best place in New York to catch foreign films, documentaries and retrospectives. Its three screens are open 365 days a year and are often among the first places in the country to show independent and foreign films. The tripped-out red-and-blue lobby is the result of a recent renovation that also gave the place new lighting and Dolby Digital Sound. Film Forum is a not-for-profit organization, which means the $10 you pay for your ticket is going to a good cause – the preservation of cinematic history.

number 203, map C **FILM FORUM**

ADDRESS 209 houston street, between 6th avenue and varick street **TELEPHONE** 212 727 8110 **WEBSITE** www.filmforum.com **OPENING HOURS** daily from 12.30 pm **CREDIT CARDS** visa, mastercard, amex **PRICE** $10 **SUBWAY** 1, 9 to houston street

ADDRESS from 59th street to 110th street, between 5th and 8th avenues **TELEPHONE** 212 360 3456
WEBSITE www.centralpark.org

CENTRAL PARK number 204, map A

There is so much to do in Central Park that it's impossible to try to do it all in one trip. Some of the park's highlights include the Belvedere (a castle built in 1865 on the park's highest point), the Dairy (a 19th-century style building housing a visitor's center and reference library), the Carousel (originally opened in 1871 and once powered by a blind mule and a horse on a treadmill in an underground pit), the formal Conservatory Garden (home to 20,000 spring tulips) and the ornamental Bethesda Fountain and "Angel of Waters" sculpture. With this list in hand, you're ready to start your urban ramble.

notes

OVERVIEW MAP NEW YORK

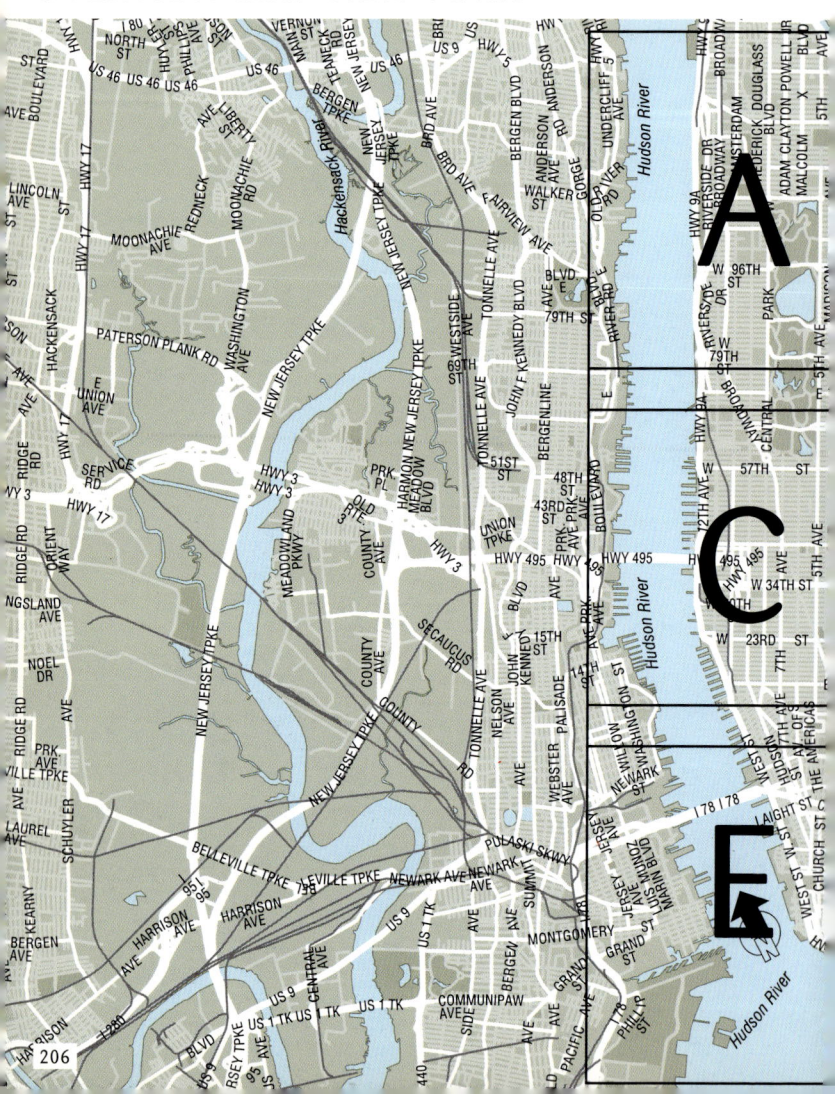

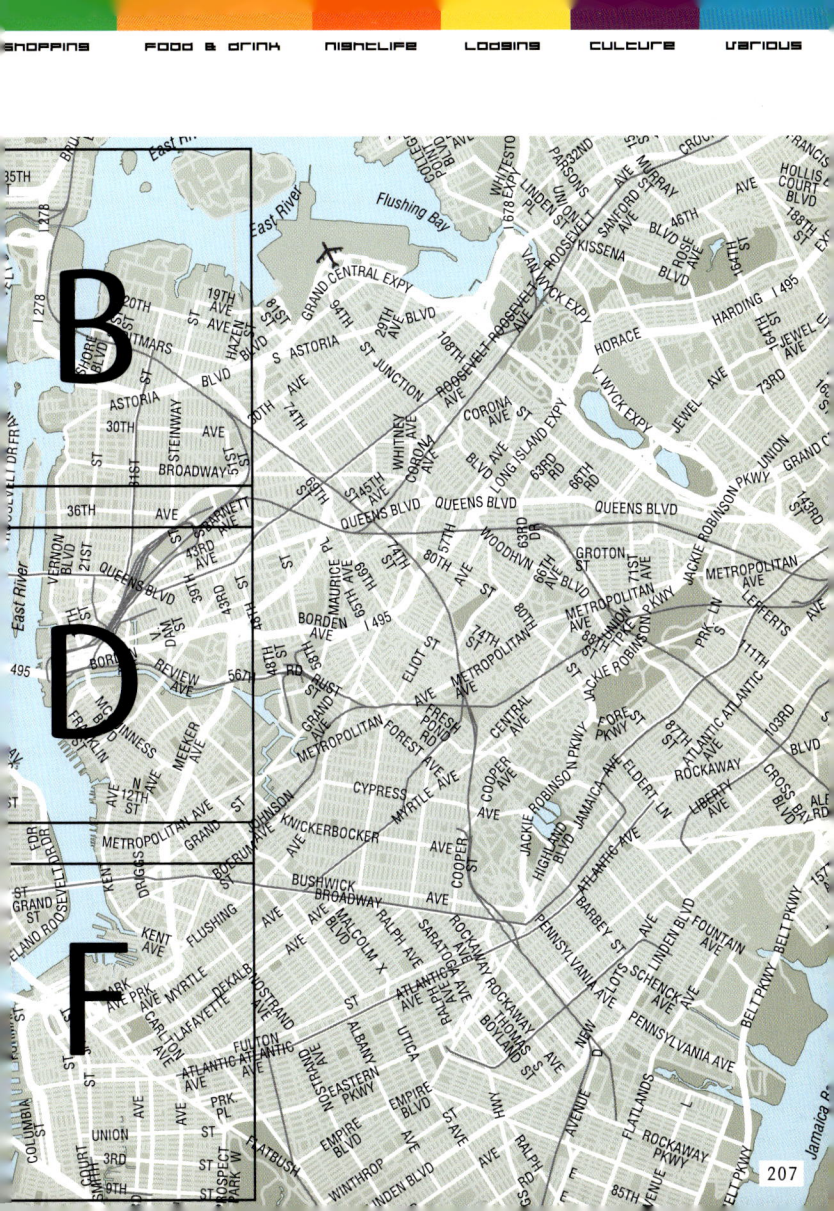

| shopping | food & drink | nightlife | lodging | culture | various |

B
D
F

207

MAP A

MAP B

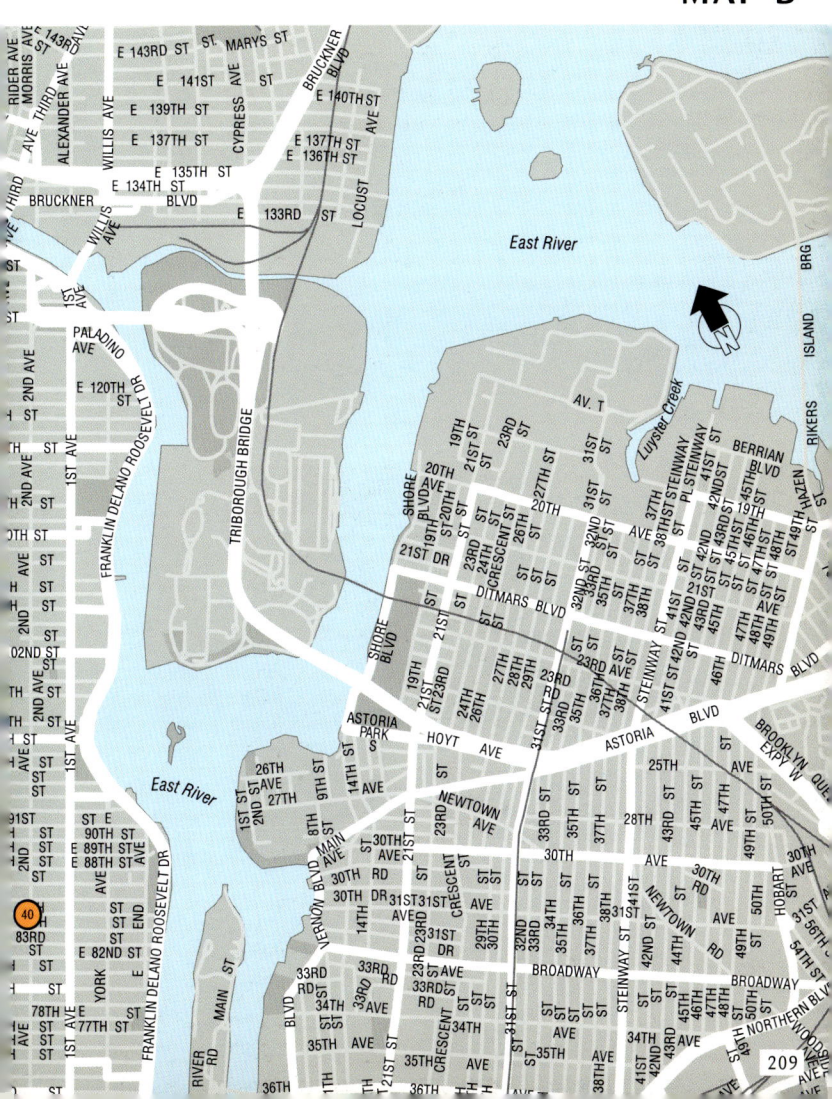

MAP C

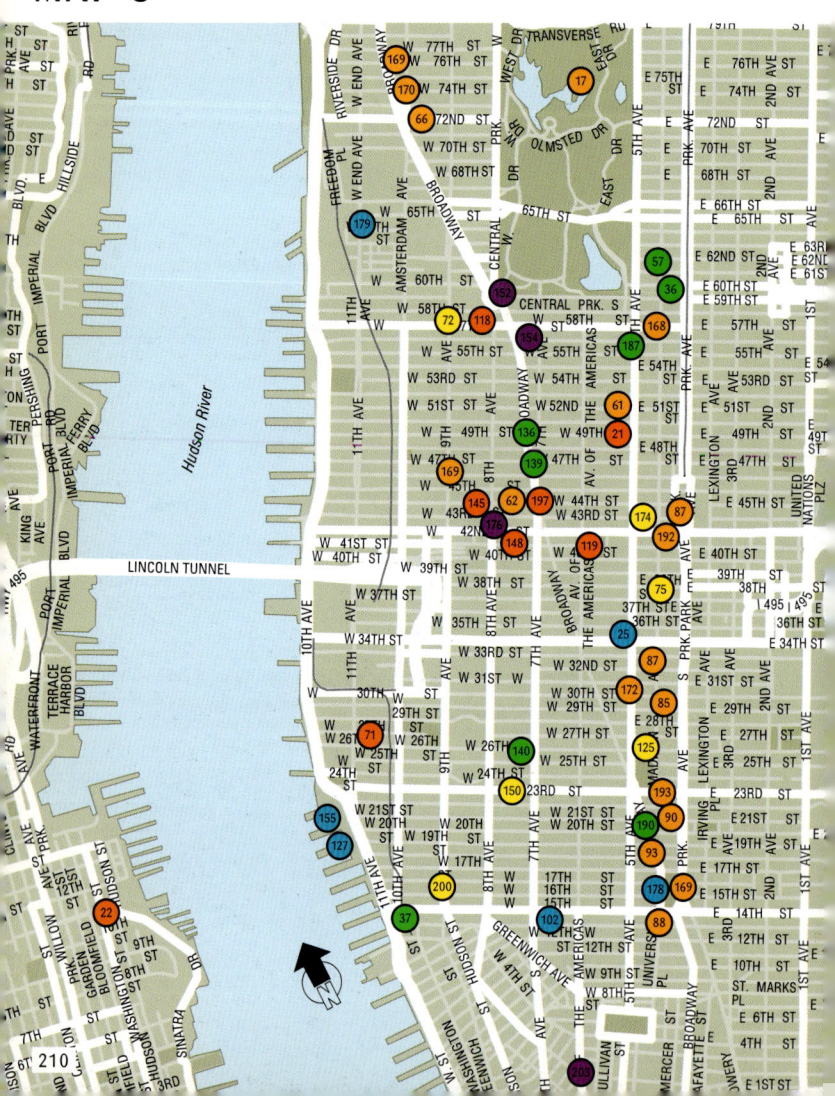

MAP D

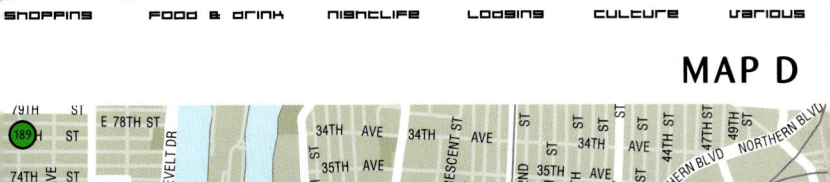

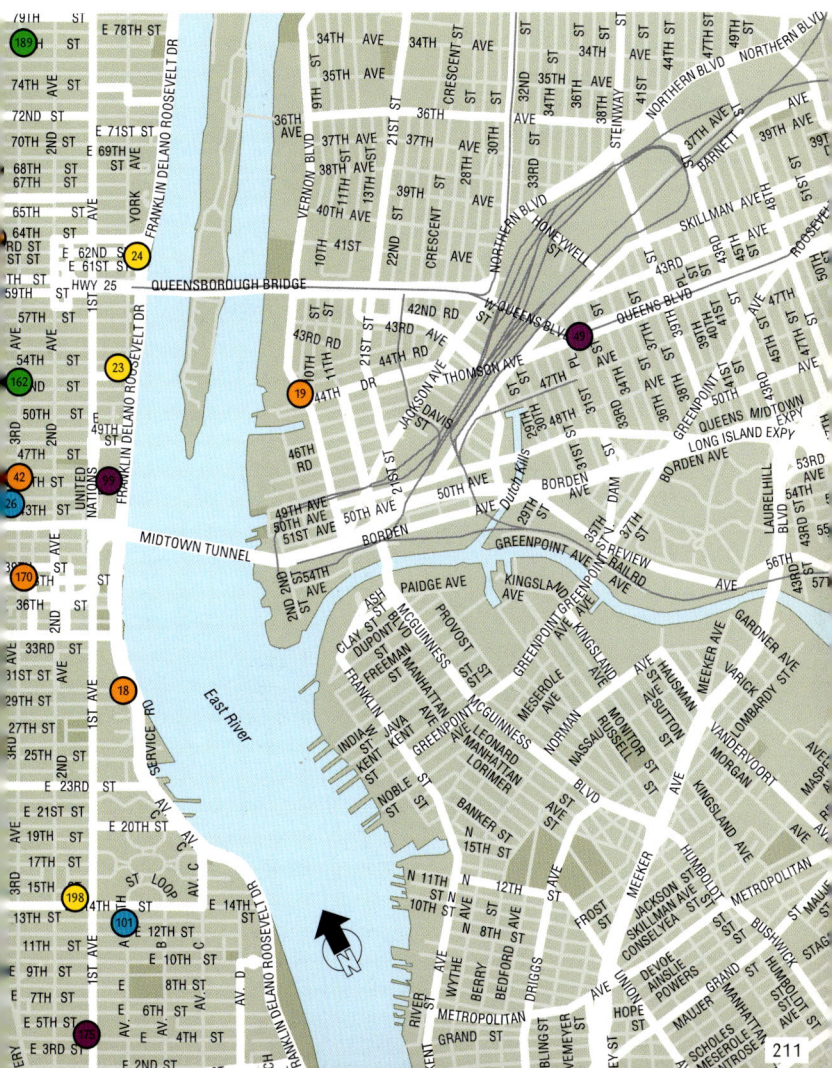

MAP E

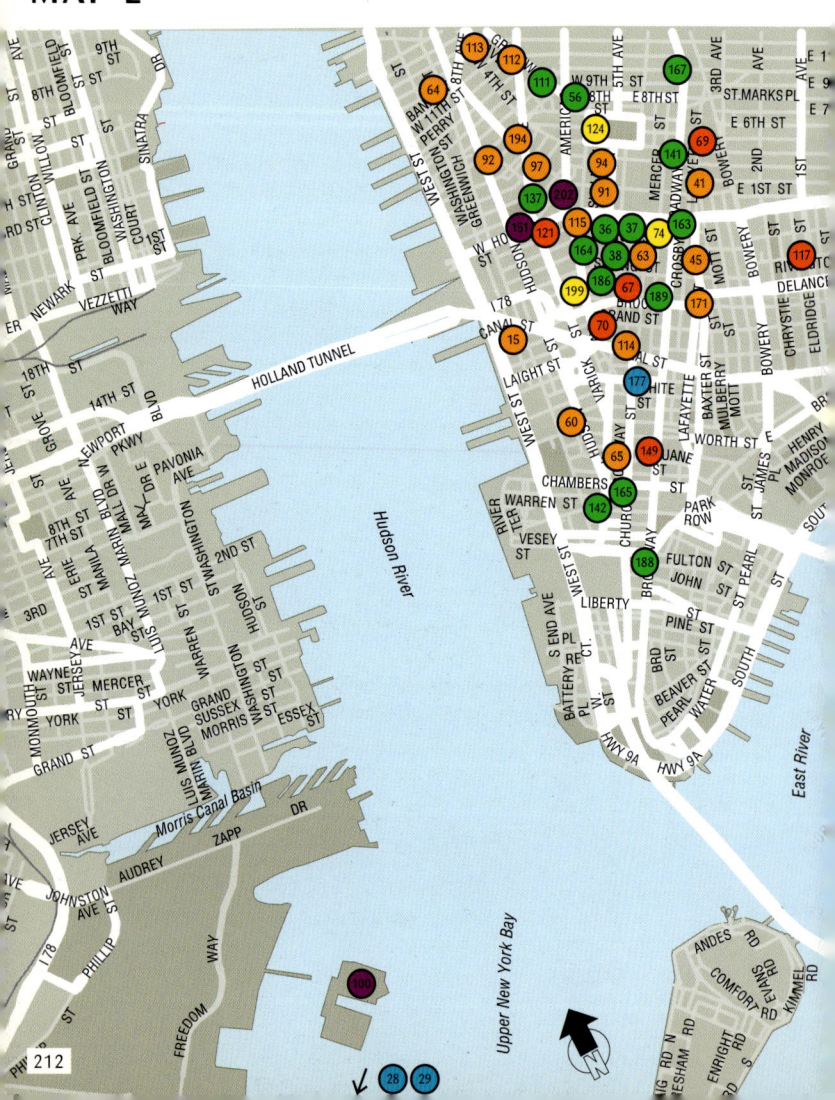

212

MAP F

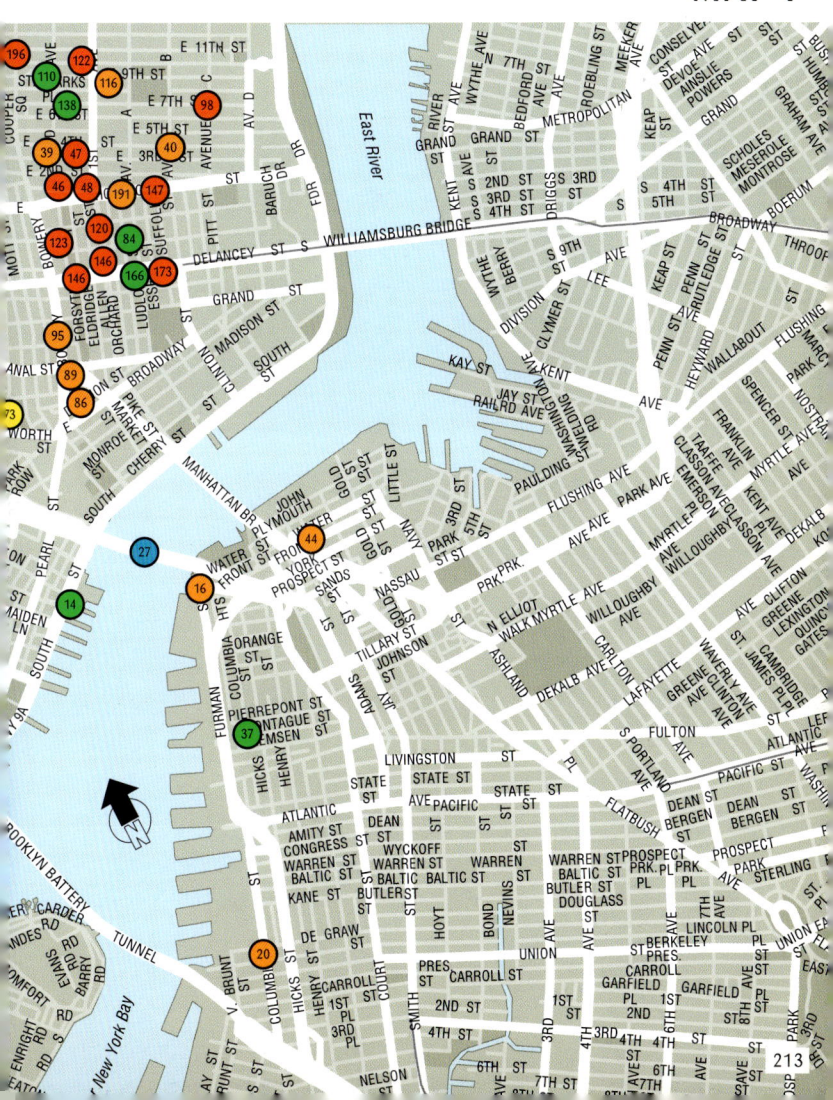

CATEGORY INDEX

CULTURE

apollo theater	153
carnegie hall	154
ellis island immigration museum	100
film forum	203
guggenheim museum	126
harlem spirituals	176
jazz at lincoln center	152
jivamukti	175
metropolitan museum	201
moma qns	49
sobs	151
united nations	99
whitney museum	202

FOOD & DRINK

"21" club	61
212	43
aix	195
alma	20
balthazar	63
b-bar & grill	39
bistrot margot	45
boat house in central park	17
chumley's	194
cub room café	115
doma café and gallery	112
dosirak	88
dt/ut	40
f. illi ponte	15
golden krust bakery	87
gramercy tavern	193
grand central oyster bar	192
gray's papaya	66
hangawi	172
havana central	93
il cortile	95
josie's	170
kati roll company	94
katz's deli	191
la pizza fresca	90
lenox lounge	144
les halles	59
lucky strike	114
magnolia bakery	113
miss maude's spoonbread too	96
new york noodletown	86
nl	91
noho star	41
odeon	65
oms/b	42
pastis	64
river café	16
sardi's	62
smoke	143
spring street natural	171
stingy lulu's	116
superfine	44
surya	97
sweet 'n' tart	89
tabla	85
tao	168
thali	92
tom's restaurant	67
tribeca grill	60
water club	18
water's edge	19
zen palate	169

LODGING

60 thompson	199
beekman tower hotel	23
bentley hotel	24
gershwin hotel	125
hotel chelsea	150
hudson hotel	72
inn at irving place	76
library hotel	174
maritime hotel	200
mercer hotel	74
morgans hotel	75
rose center for earth and space	77
second home on second avenue	198
tribeca grand hotel	73
washington square hotel	124

NIGHTLIFE

17 home	123
angel's share	196
bb kings	148
birdland	145
bob	120
bowery ballroom	146
bungalow 8	71
café carlyle	68
cbgb-omfug	46
cellar bar	119
culture club	121
d.b.a.	48
grand bar and lounge	70
howard johnson's	197
joe's pub	69
kgb	47
knitting factory	149
library bar	118
maxwell's	22
mercury lounge	147
people	117
rainbow room	21
rififi	122
verlaine	173
zum schneider	98

SHOPPING

abc carpet and home	190
barneys new york	57
bell bates natural foods	165
c.o. bigelow apothecaries	56
century 21	188
christian louboutin	58
colony music center	136
dkny	36
dwr (design within reach)	37
henri bendel	187
jazz record center	140
kirna zabete	38
lafco new york	163
laina jane	111
moo shoes	166
other music	141
quest bookshop	162
russ & daughters	84
sam ash music	139
scoop	189
shu uemura	164
south street seaport	14
st. mark's bookstore	110
stern's music	142
steven alan	186
vinylmania	137
wholesome market	167
wowsville	138
maximus soho	177
sahara east	101
savory sojourns	102
statue of liberty	28
toga bike shop	179
turntables on the hudson	155

VARIOUS

acqua beauty bar	178
brooklyn bridge	27
central park	204
chelsea piers	127
chrysler building	26
empire state building	25
great kills park	29
hurry date	128

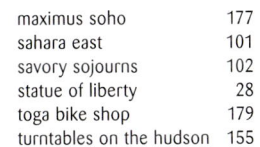

215

ALPHABETICAL INDEX

17 home	123
"21" club	61
60 thompson	199
212	43

A
abc carpet and home	190
acqua beauty bar	178
aix	195
alma	20
angel's share	196
apollo theater	153

B
balthazar	63
barneys new york	57
bb kings	148
b-bar & grill	39
beekman tower hotel	23
bell bates natural foods	165
bentley hotel	24
birdland	145
bistrot margot	45
boat house in central park	17
bob	120
bowery ballroom	146
brooklyn bridge	27
bungalow 8	71

C
c.o. bigelow apothecaries	56
café carlyle	68
carnegie hall	154
cbgb-omfug	46
cellar bar	119
central park	204
century 21	188
chelsea piers	127
christian louboutin	58
chrysler building	26
chumley's	194
colony music center	136
cub room café	115
culture club	121

D
d.b.a.	48
dkny	36
doma café and gallery	112
dosirak	88
dt/ut	40
dwr (design within reach)	37

E
ellis island immigration museum	100
empire state building	25

F
f. illi ponte	15
film forum	203

G
gershwin hotel	125
golden krust bakery	87
gramercy tavern	193
grand bar and lounge	70
grand central oyster bar	192
gray's papaya	66
great kills park	29
guggenheim museum	126

H
hangawi	172
harlem spiritiuals	176
havana central	93
henri bendel	187
hotel chelsea	150
howard johnson's	197
hudson hotel	72
hurry date	128

I
il cortile	95
inn at irving place	76

J
jazz at lincoln center	152
jazz record center	140
jivamukti	175
joe's pub	69
josie's	170

K
kati roll company	94
katz's deli	191
kgb	47
kirna zabete	38
knitting factory	149

L
la pizza fresca	90
lafco new york	163
laina jane	111
lenox lounge	144
les halles	59
library bar	118
library hotel	174
lucky strike	114

M
magnolia bakery	113
maritime hotel	200
maximus soho	177
maxwell's	22
mercer hotel	74
mercury lounge	147
metropolitan museum	201
miss maude's spoon bread too	96

216

moma qns	49
moo shoes	166
morgans hotel	75

N
new york noodletown	86
nl	91
noho star	41

O
odeon	65
oms/b	42
other music	141

P
pastis	64
people	117

Q
quest bookshop	162

R
rainbow room	21
rififi	122
river café	16
rose center for earth and space	77
russ & daughters	84

S
sahara east	101
sam ash music	139
sardi's	62
savory sojourns	102
scoop	189
second home on second avenue	198
shu uemura	164
smoke	143
sobs	151
south street seaport	14
spring street natural	171
st. mark's bookstore	110
statue of liberty	28
stern's music	142
steven alan	186
stingy lulu's	116
superfine	44
surya	97
sweet 'n' tart	89

T
tabla	85
tao	168
thali	92
toga bike shop	179
tom's restaurant	67
tribeca grand hotel	73
tribeca grill	60
turntables on the hudson	155

U
united nations	99

V
verlaine	173
vinylmania	137

W
washington square hotel	124
water club	18
water's edge	19
whitney museum	202
wholesome market	167
wowsville	138

Z
zen palate	169
zum schneider	98

notes

notes

notes

notes

Manhattan Subway Map

MTA New York City Transit
February 2004

Please check our website **www.mta.info** often for latest service changes.

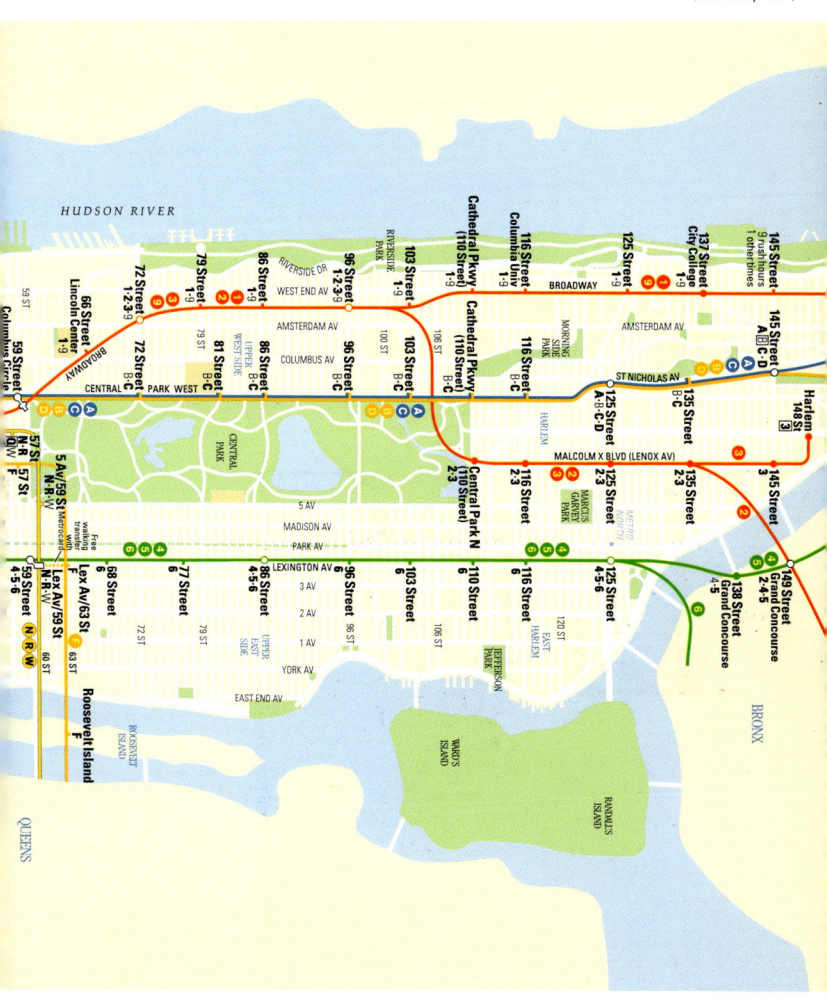

(turn map 90°)

HUDSON RIVER

145 Street
9 rush hrs
1 other times

137 Street
City College
1·9

125 Street
1·9

116 Street
Columbia Univ
1·9

Cathedral Pkwy
(110 Street)
1·9

103 Street
1·9

96 Street
1·2·3·9

86 Street
1·9

79 Street
1·9

72 Street
1·2·3

66 Street
Lincoln Center
1·9

59 Street
Columbus Circle
1·9

RIVERSIDE DR
RIVERSIDE PARK
WEST END AV
BROADWAY

145 Street
A B C D

St Nicholas AV

135 Street
B·C

125 Street
A·B·C·D

116 Street
B·C

Cathedral Pkwy
(110 Street)
B·C

103 Street
B·C

96 Street
B·C

86 Street
B·C

81 Street
B·C

72 Street
B·C

AMSTERDAM AV
COLUMBUS AV
CENTRAL PARK WEST

MORNINGSIDE PARK
HARLEM
UPPER WEST SIDE

59 St
57 St
N·R
Q·V
57 St
F
5 Av/59 St
N·R·W
free walking transfer
Lex Av/63 St
F
60 ST
Roosevelt Island
F

CENTRAL PARK

Harlem 148 St
3

135 Street
2·3

Malcolm X Blvd (Lenox Av)

125 Street
2·3

116 Street
2·3

Central Park N
(110 Street)
2·3

5 AV
MADISON AV
PARK AV
LEXINGTON AV
3 AV
2 AV
1 AV
YORK AV
EAST END AV

68 Street
6

77 Street
6

86 Street
4·5·6

96 Street
6

103 Street
6

110 Street
6

116 Street
6

125 Street
4·5·6

59 Street
4·5·6

MARCUS GARVEY PARK
EAST HARLEM
JEFFERSON PARK

METRO NORTH

149 Street
Grand Concourse
2·4·5

138 Street
Grand Concourse
4·5

BRONX

WARD'S ISLAND
RANDALL'S ISLAND
ROOSEVELT ISLAND
QUEENS

223

ALSO AVAILABLE

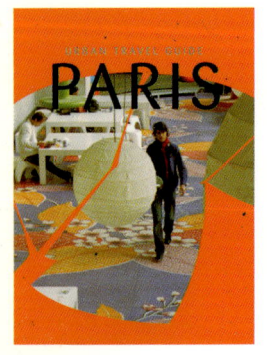

URBAN TRAVEL GUIDE
PARIS
isbn 90-5767-125-5

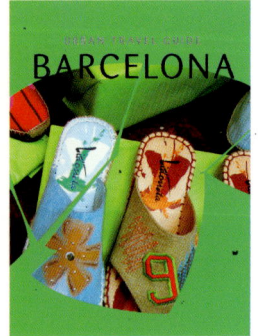

URBAN TRAVEL GUIDE
BARCELONA
isbn 90-5767-128-X

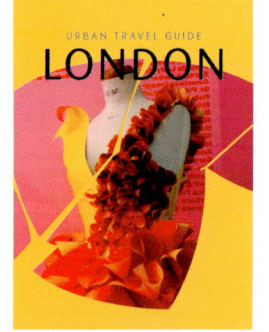

URBAN TRAVEL GUIDE
LONDON
isbn 90-5767-127-1

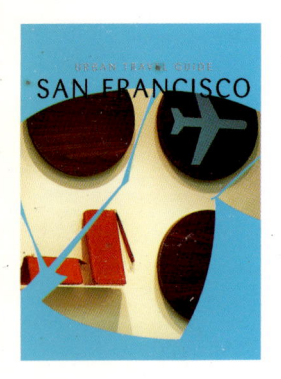

URBAN TRAVEL GUIDE
SAN FRANCISCO
isbn 90-5767-126-3